The Days of My Appointed Time

Expectant Christian Living in an Uncertain World

by

Floyd Bland

Copyright © 2025 by Floyd Bland, all rights reserved.

Reproduction, transmission, or storage of any part of this book is prohibited, except for brief quotations used in critical reviews or other permitted noncommercial uses under U.S. copyright law.

This inspirational Christian book strives for factual accuracy. It is not intended as a substitute for professional or legal advice. The publisher and author disclaim all liability for errors or omissions in the content.

Certain names and events have been changed for the sake of anonymity. Any resemblance to actual persons, living or dead, or to real events or locations is purely coincidental.

Passages marked (AKJV) are Scripture quotations from The Authorized (King James) Version. Rights in the Authorized Version in the United Kingdom are vested in the Crown. Reproduced by permission of the Crown's patentee, Cambridge University Press.

All other Scripture will be taken from the New King James Version®. Copyright © 1982 by Thomas Nelson. Used by permission. All rights reserved.

All trademarks, service marks, and other proprietary rights referenced in this book are the property of their respective owners.

ISBN: 978-1-7325342-7-8

Library of Congress Control Number: 2025904264

I Wait, Till My Change Come!

Contents

With Gratitude — vi

Introduction
Three Paradigms for Christian Perseverance — 1

Chapter One
Eagerly Expecting Our Divine Transformation — 7

Chapter Two
Yearning for Christ and the Change He Brings — 29

Chapter Three
Waiting on God's Appointed Time for Change — 67

Chapter Four
Preparing for the Change God Has for Us — 100

About the Author — 140

With Gratitude

With each passing day, I grow increasingly grateful to God for His love, mercy, and the second chances granted through our Lord Jesus Christ.

I am deeply grateful for my beloved family, whose unwavering love and constant encouragement have been an enduring source of strength throughout my years of service to Christ.

I am also grateful to Susan Robitaille of Second Look Editorial Services and Paramita Bhattacharjee of Creative Paramita Book Cover Designs for their expertise in preparing and designing this book for publication.

Introduction

Introduction
Three Paradigms for Christian Perseverance

Job's Captivating Story

Job is a righteous man who faces intense personal and physical hardships. Satan, with God's permission, tests him to prove his faith and character—he has lost his children, possessions, and health. Job's three friends come to sympathize and comfort him but insist that his suffering must be punishment for sin.

Throughout their debates, Job maintains his innocence while exploring the nature of human suffering and challenging the character of God.

The Lord responds from a whirlwind, revealing how limited human understanding is in contrast to His infinite wisdom. Job subsequently repents for challenging God, and as a result, the Lord restores twice the wealth and children he had lost.

Job shares his view of the grave (Sheol), consistent with the broader Old Testament perspective: a place of separation, where the dead no longer interact with the living.

However, Job also hints at the potential for renewal or change beyond the grave, expressing deep longing for hope in his suffering:

> If a man die, shall he live *again*? All the days of my appointed time will I wait, till my change come. Job 14:14 (AKJV)

Although Job 14:14 was written for an Old Testament audience, it offers three enduring paradigms for Christian perseverance for our New Testament Age.

➢ *My Appointed Time.*
The Hebrew *tsaba* (or *saba*) (Strong's OT 6635), translated as "fighting," "war," "army," "host," "company," or "service," emphasizes the concept of being strategically organized for warfare. It symbolizes a time dedicated to fulfilling military service and can imply a time of non-military service to the Lord.[1]

In the Old Testament, the word can describe either military service or the armies of Israel (Numbers 1:3, 1 Samuel 17:55), God's heavenly angelic host (1 Kings 22:19), or the Levites serving in the tabernacle. (Numbers 8:24) However, in the book of Job, it describes a prolonged, dedicated time of "hard service."

Juxtaposing a life defined by the rigid constraints and hardships of military service with the joyful anticipation of a dynamic transformation upon release, "all the days of my appointed time" refers to the timeframe until the long-awaited, cherished goal can be realized.

➢ *I Will Wait.*
The Hebrew *yachal* (Strong's OT 3176), translated as "to wait," "hope," or "trust," carries a sense of confident expectation. It is not about vague hopes

or hollow aspirations, but, as one author observes, it is a "solid ground of expectation for the righteous. As such it is directed towards God."[2]

The term is often used where there is a hopeful anticipation for good, reflecting a steadfast trust in God's perfect timing and faithfulness. It suggests a calm, patient confidence that the Lord will act, especially during times of uncertainty or peril.

The idea of waiting is essential to our Christian faith, as the Lord delights in our trust that He will fulfill His precious promises. In particular, we eagerly await the glorious fulfillment of His promise of a new heaven and earth. In this waiting, our faith is neither futile nor irrelevant; instead, our waiting reflects an authentic trust in a living God.

➢ *Till My Change Come.*
The Hebrew *chaliphah* (Strong's OT 2487), translated as "pass on," "pass away," "pass through," "change," "exchange," "alter," or "renew," conveys the idea of changing from one thing to another. It can refer to a change in clothing (Genesis 45:22) or a change in personnel. (1 Kings 5:14) Here, it suggests a transformation in circumstances associated with God's blessing—a shift from one state to another, for the better, as one thing is exchanged for another.[3]

In summary, we live purposeful lives—active and expectant—eagerly anticipating God's ultimate transformation. We do not spend our time in passivity, but in a joyful odyssey that culminates when He trades our present trials for eternal glory.

Anchored by our unwavering faith in God's precious and enduring promises—abundant life now and eternal life to come—we live with purpose and hope, embracing the present while anticipating the glory ahead, even amid a troubled world steeped in skepticism.

Although Job 14:14 serves as the central text of this book, the following excerpts of Moses' prayer in Psalm 90 also inspired me to write it:

> Lord, You have been our dwelling place in all generations. Before the mountains were brought forth, Or ever You had formed the earth and the world, Even from everlasting to everlasting, You *are* God.
>
> The days of our lives *are* seventy years; And if by reason of strength *they are* eighty years, Yet their boast *is* only labor and sorrow; For it is soon cut off, and we fly away. . . . So teach *us* to number our days, That we may gain a heart of wisdom.   Psalm 90: 1–2, 10, 12

In the following pages, we will explore Job's paradigms for Christian perseverance as we expect, desire, await, and prepare for the glorious change that awaits us.

Notes

[1]See: John E. Hartley, "1865 צָבָא (ṣābāʾ) fight, serve," in *Theological Wordbook of the Old Testament*, ed. R. Laird Harris, Gleason L. Archer Jr., and Bruce K. Waltke, vol. 2, 2nd printing (Chicago: Moody Press, 1981), 749–50; Otto Zöckler, "The Book of Job," trans. L. J. Evans, vol. 8 of *Lange's Commentary on the Holy Scriptures*, 7th printing (Grand Rapids: Zondervan, 1980), 412; Franz Delitzsch, *Biblical Commentary on the Book of Job*, vol. 4 of *Commentary on the Old Testament*, reprint (Grand Rapids: Eerdmans, 1986), 231.

[2]See: Paul R. Gilchrist, "859 יָחַל (yāḥal) wait, hope," in *Theological Wordbook of the Old Testament*, ed. R. Laird Harris, Gleason L. Archer Jr., and Bruce K. Waltke, vol. 1, 2nd printing (Chicago: Moody Press, 1981), 373; "3176. יָחַל yāḥal)," in *The Complete Word Study Dictionary: Old Testament*, Word Study Series, by Warren Baker and Eugene Carpenter (Chattanooga, TN: AMG Publishers, 2003), 443–44.

[3]See: Laird R. Harris, "666 חָלַף (ḥālap) pass on, or away, pass through, change," in *Theological Wordbook of the Old Testament*, ed. R. Laird Harris, Gleason L. Archer Jr., and Bruce K. Waltke, vol. 1, 2nd printing (Chicago: Moody Press, 1981), 291–92; William Wilson, "Change," in *Wilson's Old Testament Word Studies*, unabridged (Peabody, MA: Hendrickson Publishers, 1990), 72.

Chapter One

Chapter One
Eagerly Expecting Our Divine Transformation

Our Unshakable Hope and Purpose
Christians expect profound change, both in our present spiritual growth and in the glorious future that awaits us. Thus, transformation is not merely a distant hope; it is also a present, living reality. God is at work inside us, shaping our lives, renewing our faith, and refining our character.

We live with unshakable hope and purpose, eagerly awaiting the glorious future He has promised. His Holy Spirit continues the work of transformation and renewal from within.

As we reflect on God's precious promises, we find security in His faithfulness. His Holy Spirit, who dwells within us, empowers us to persevere through life's challenges, guiding us with His amazing power and grace.

God's perfect plan inspires our complete trust and confident anticipation as we look toward the blessed, eternal future He has prepared for us.

God's Design: Our Blessed Eternal Future
Many today refer to God with vague terms like "the universe," or informal phrases such as "the man upstairs," which fall woefully short of the reverence, awe, and respect our Lord deserves.

It is impossible to describe God as we describe inanimate objects or created beings. The Scriptures tell us that in Him we "live and move and have our being." (Acts 17:28) Although we only "know in part" (1 Corinthians 13:9), every question finds its answer in Him and every problem its solution. Thus, we define God as follows:

> We believe that there is one, and only one, living and true God, an infinite, intelligent Spirit, the Maker and Supreme Ruler of heaven and earth; inexpressibly glorious in holiness, and worthy of all possible honor, confidence, and love; that in the unity of the Godhead there are three persons, the Father, the Son, and the Holy Ghost; equal in every divine perfection, and executing distinct and harmonious offices in the great work of redemption.[1]

In both the Authorized and New King James Bibles, the divine name YHWH is rendered in all caps as LORD, distinguishing it from "Lord" (Adonai}. God used its derivative, "I Am that I Am," when He called Moses to free the children of Israel from Egyptian bondage. (Exodus 3:14)[2]

So sacred is His name that when the Lord Jesus Christ applied the term "I Am" to Himself as the Son of God, He incited the rage of His audience. (John 8:54–59)

His incomparable majesty and splendor are beyond human comprehension, just as Job observed:

> Therefore I have uttered what I did not understand, Things too wonderful for me, which I did not know. Job 42:3b

Yet, in His grace, He chooses to reveal Himself to us as Infinite, Eternal, Immutable, Omniscient, Omnipotent, True and Righteous, Loving, and Holy. Through these distinct attributes, we can begin to experience His presence and purpose for our lives.

➤ *Infinite*

God is limitless in power, knowledge, and presence. He is present everywhere at all times, and His omnipresence fills heaven and earth without diminishing His essence. He exists beyond all we can comprehend, as the Psalmist declares:

> Great *is* our Lord, and mighty in power; His understanding *is* infinite. Psalm 147:5

➤ *Eternal*

God exists outside the constraints of time and space. He has no beginning and no end. He is the Everlasting God. As one theologian notes:

> With Him there is no distinction between the present, past, and future; but all things

are equally and always present to Him. With Him duration is an eternal now.³

➢ *Immutable*

God does not change. He is the same yesterday, today, and forever. Unlike humans, He does not vacillate or shift with popular opinion or market trends. He remains steadfast and sure. He is absolutely perfect and requires no improvement:

> For I *am* the Lord, I do not change; Therefore you are not consumed, O sons of Jacob. Malachi 3:6

➢ *Omniscient*

God possesses complete, eternal knowledge. He is all-wise, and nothing is hidden from His sight. He knows all that is, has been, and will be, both actual and possible, past, present, or future:

> For *as* the heavens are higher than the earth, So are My ways higher than your ways, And My thoughts than your thoughts. Isaiah 55:9

➢ *Omnipotent*

God's power is absolute to do anything He wills, and His will is always aligned with His perfect nature. He is the self-existent origin of all life as the Living God. He is the Creator, Sustainer, and Sovereign Ruler of heaven and earth:

> When Abram was ninety-nine years old, the LORD appeared to Abram and said to him, "I *am* Almighty God; walk before Me and be blameless." Genesis 17:1

> ➢ *True and Righteous*

God embodies truth and faithfulness as the very standard of moral integrity. His judgments are just, His promises unshakable, and His unwavering character inspires our unwavering trust:

> Therefore know that the LORD your God, He *is* God, the faithful God who keeps covenant and mercy for a thousand generations with those who love Him and keep His commandments. Deuteronomy 7:9

> The works of His hands *are* verity and justice; All His precepts *are* sure. They stand fast forever and ever, *And are* done in truth and uprightness. He has sent redemption to His people; He has commanded His covenant forever: Holy and awesome *is* His name. Psalm 111:7–9

➢ *Love*

God's eternal, deliberate, selfless, and sacrificial plan for our benefit, defines love. He continually reveals His heart through countless expressions of benevolence each day. Yet, His greatest demonstration was in the giving of His Son to forgive our sin and restore our fellowship forever:

> He who does not love does not know God, for God is love. . . . In this is love, not that we loved God, but that He loved us and sent His Son *to be* the propitiation for our sins. 1 John 4:8, 10

➤ *Holy*

God is morally and spiritually perfect in all aspects. Holiness is self-affirming purity and is the very essence of His being. God alone maintains moral excellence because only He is pure, majestic, glorious, and without equal:

> Who *is* like You, O LORD, among the gods? Who *is* like You, glorious in holiness, Fearful in praises, doing wonders? Exodus 15:11

God's perfect nature assures us of His sovereign control. Because of this, we can place our full trust in Him through all of life's challenges. His presence gives us hope for present and future change, and His promises have consistently proven reliable and steadfast. Consider these two:

> God *is* not a man, that He should lie, Nor a son of man, that He should repent. Has He said, and will He not do? Or has He spoken, and will He not make it good? Numbers 23:19

> Being confident of this very thing, that He who has begun a good work in you will complete *it* until the day of Jesus Christ.
> Philippians 1:6

God is not an enigma, neither is He unknowable or unreachable. He is a personal God who desires our fellowship and has designed a plan for each of us to know and experience personally—and fully:

> For I know the thoughts that I think toward you, says the Lord, thoughts of peace and not of evil, to give you a future and a hope.
> Jeremiah 29:11

> But as it is written: "Eye has not seen, nor ear heard, Nor have entered into the heart of man The things which God has prepared for those who love Him."
> 1 Corinthians 2:9

Throughout history, we have described His character in many ways, but never as a "liar." Thus, because of His veracity and faithfulness, we can eagerly and confidently expect the Lord to fulfill every promise He has made—in *His* perfect timing.

Two Opposing Realities
Our Christian life involves two contrasting realities: the present and the future. In our present reality, God's Holy Spirit is transforming us into

Christ's likeness as we grow in faith. This is our sanctification.

Still, we have a future reality where we will share eternal glory with God. This is our complete and final transformation, when we enter our eternal home—called a new heaven and a new earth—free from sin, pain, death, and suffering. This is our glorification.

God's Holy Spirit actively guides and empowers our spiritual progression, continually shaping us to reflect the character and virtue of our Lord. This ongoing transformation prepares us for the glorious, eternal life that awaits us—far beyond anything we could hope for or imagine.

Our ultimate change will coincide with the consummation of all things—an event the world itself eagerly anticipates:

> For the earnest expectation of the creation eagerly waits for the revealing of the sons of God. For the creation was subjected to futility, not willingly, but because of Him who subjected *it* in hope; because the creation itself also will be delivered from the bondage of corruption into the glorious liberty of the children of God. For we know that the whole creation groans and labors with birth pangs together until now. Romans 8:19–22

The Spirit of Christ within us gives us hope for glory. (Colossians 1:27) He is our confidence and joyful expectation of future blessing.

Scripture declares that flesh and blood will not inherit the Kingdom of God. When our Lord calls us from labor to reward, we will experience the pinnacle of His redemptive plan where the wicked cease from troubling and the weary are at rest, as echoed in Job 3:17.

Of this glorious transformation, the Scriptures attest:

> Now this I say, brethren, that flesh and blood cannot inherit the kingdom of God; nor does corruption inherit incorruption. Behold, I tell you a mystery: We shall not all sleep, but we shall all be changed—in a moment, in the twinkling of an eye, at the last trumpet. For the trumpet will sound, and the dead will be raised incorruptible, and we shall be changed. For this corruptible must put on incorruption, and this mortal *must* put on immortality.
> 1 Corinthians 15:50–53

With new immortal bodies that resemble Christ's resurrected body, we will see Him as He is and be like Him. (1 John 3:2) As our Christian journey unfolds, we remain grounded in the "here and now," while anxiously looking forward to the blessed future that lies before us.

Anxiously Looking Forward
Unfortunately, our pilgrimage takes place in the "Last Days," when the Enemy is deceiving many into prioritizing the material and temporal over the spiritual and eternal:

> But know this, that in the last days perilous times will come: For men will be lovers of themselves, lovers of money, boasters, proud, blasphemers, disobedient to parents, unthankful, unholy, unloving, unforgiving, slanderers, without self-control, brutal, despisers of good, traitors, headstrong, haughty, lovers of pleasure rather than lovers of God, having a form of godliness but denying its power. And from such people turn away . . . always learning and never able to come to the knowledge of the truth.
> 2 Timothy 3:1–4, 7

Far too often, we ignore God's Word and its teachings by trivializing our God-given human dignity. This disregard is reflected in how we have reduced it to mere market value. This violation of our human worth is reflected in the killing of the unborn and vulnerable, the euthanasia of older adults and the infirm, and the exploitation, trafficking, abuse, and violence committed against innocent lives.

Many of us live as if we will never die, but such thinking is illusory. Scripture tells us that the typical human lifespan is seventy to eighty years, more or less. Yet, in the grand scope of eternity, this life is but a fleeting "blink of an eye." Since we cannot leave this earth alive, nor can we take any personal possessions with us, it would be prudent to make plans for our souls now to avoid eternal peril:

> For what is a man profited, if he shall gain the whole world, and lose his own soul? or what shall a man give in exchange for his soul? Matthew 16:26

My Christian pilgrimage has been both eventful and profoundly fulfilling, beginning as a youth in the early sixties and continuing through my years of ministry. However, I have come to realize that my heavenly homesickness intensifies with each passing year.

Thus, Job's poignant words resonate with me more today than ever before:

> I know *that* my Redeemer lives, And He shall stand at last on the earth; And after my skin is destroyed, this *I know,* That in my flesh I shall see God, Whom I shall see for myself, And my eyes shall behold, and not another. *How* my heart yearns within me!
> Job 19:25–27

Job's famous declaration is one of the most powerful and hopeful in the Bible as it reveals his unwavering faith in God, despite his overwhelming circumstances. In the midst of suffering and uncertainty, Job declares an unwavering hope for redemption—a defining moment of faith amid despair. His hope of a bodily resurrection foreshadows our ultimate hope fulfilled in Christ.

Job is asserting that even when everything seems lost, it is possible to finish well, and see God prevail. With that same faith, I, too, desire to finish well by living out the principles of Psalm 92:14 (AKJV):

> They shall still bring forth fruit in old age;
> they shall be fat and flourishing.

I will not achieve total perfection in this life—I am still learning and growing. But I have the perfect example in Christ, whose Holy Spirit empowers me to "press on" each day.

I "press on" toward the heavenly prize, awaiting all who love His appearing. (Philippians 3:14, 2 Timothy 4:8) Although the "outer man" continues to decay, the Holy Spirit renews and strengthens the "inner man" to persevere. (2 Corinthians 4:16)

Mine has been an awesome Christian journey, for there has never been a time when He was not with me, even when I was not aware of His presence and providence, showing Himself to be my wonderful Keeper, Friend, Provider, and Redeemer.

> ➤ *Keeper*

Psalm 121:5 identifies the Lord as my Keeper, while 1 Peter 1:5 assures me that I am kept by the power of God through faith unto salvation.

I cannot recall the exact moment when I accepted Christ as my personal Savior and Lord. We were a loving Christian family, and my parents instilled in me a desire to love the Lord at an early age, to which I responded with fervor and sincerity.

What I can say is that more than half a century has passed, and both my love for and commitment to the Lord remain vibrant. I cannot take credit for this; His Holy Spirit kept me. There were times when I wanted to pause or quit the journey, yet He always prompted me to continue:

> I have been crucified with Christ; it is no longer I who live, but Christ lives in me; and the *life* which I now live in the flesh I live by faith in the Son of God, who loved me and gave Himself for me.
> Galatians 2:20

> ➤ *Friend*

Not only is He our Keeper, but He is also our close Friend, as described in Proverbs 18:24. Before leaving His Disciples, Jesus affirmed His role as Friend. (John 15:14–15) In times of loneliness and doubt, He is a kind, compassionate Friend who calms my fears and lifts my broken spirit. He walks with me through adversity, sickness, sorrow, and loss—bringing peace and comfort as He promised:

> Yea, though I walk through the valley of the shadow of death, I will fear no evil; For You *are* with me; Your rod and Your staff, they comfort me.   Psalm 23:4

> For His anger *is but for* a moment, His favor *is for* life; Weeping may endure for a night, But joy *comes* in the morning.
>   Psalm 30:5

➢ *Provider*

God is my Provider, who faithfully supplies the air I breathe, the food I eat, the clothes I wear, and the health and strength that shows His loving care. God's blessings reach far beyond material needs, fostering contentment, and unwavering hope in times of uncertainty. Reflecting on what He has done for me inspires peace and joy, strengthening my trust in Him for both present and future circumstances:

> You will keep *him* in perfect peace, *Whose* mind *is* stayed *on You,* Because he trusts in You.   Isaiah 26:3

When I genuinely follow the advice of my spiritual leaders—who have often told me to "let go and let God"—I surrender to Him and trust Him completely. In doing so, He constantly proves that He is fully aware of my needs and desires to provide for them in His perfect timing:

> And my God shall supply all your need according to His riches in glory by Christ Jesus.   Philippians 4:19

➢ *Redeemer*

I met the Redeemer when I came to understand that sin is not only a global plague, but also a personal one. Before Christ, my spiritual condition was total ruin, and I needed a Savior. I saw my condition and cried out to God:

> O wretched man that I am! Who will deliver me from this body of death?
>   Romans 7:24

I could never measure up to the perfection in Jesus Christ, for my righteousness was as worthless as "filthy rags." (Isaiah 64:6) I was under God's just condemnation to eternal ruin—without defense or excuse. I needed Jesus Christ as my Savior and Redeemer, because I could not stand before God on my own merit. However, the Lord promised that my new life was possible:

> Blessed *are* the poor in spirit, For theirs is the kingdom of heaven. Blessed *are* those

who mourn, For they shall be comforted. .
. . Blessed *are* those who hunger and thirst
for righteousness, For they shall be filled.
Matthew 5:3–4, 6

In humble submission—with my whole heart—I turned to Jesus Christ as my personal Lord and Savior and was Born Again. At that precise moment, His Holy Spirit "quickened" me, and I was spiritually changed forever.

Forever Changed Through Christ
Some say rightly that the distance between heaven and hell is approximately twelve to eighteen inches, or the distance between the head and the heart. More than mere intellectual assent, I opened my heart to Christ, and He transformed me into His new creation:

> Therefore, if anyone is in Christ, he is a new creation; old things have passed away; behold, all things have become new. 2 Corinthians 5:17

It was as if God the Holy Spirit turned on a "no longer dead but alive" switch inside me. This spiritual change was unlike anything I will ever know or experience in this life again, and I came to know the abundant life Jesus promises:

> The thief does not come except to steal, and to kill, and to destroy. I have come

> that they may have life, and that they may have it more abundantly. John 10:10

The "Born Again" experience changed my spiritual makeup while also securing my access to God's glorious Kingdom forever. (John 3:3) In this regeneration, I received a completely new spiritual nature.[4]

Some reduce the New Birth to material blessing, but this overlooks the very heart of the transformation—for God's Kingdom is spiritual, not material. His perfect will is our complete inner transformation. Some of us may attain fame, fortune, and influence in this life, while others may not. Yet, all of us matter to God:

> For you see your calling, brethren, that not many wise according to the flesh, not many mighty, not many noble, are called. But God has chosen the foolish things of the world to put to shame the wise, and God has chosen the weak things of the world to put to shame the things which are mighty; and the base things of the world and the things which are despised God has chosen, and the things which are not, to bring to nothing the things that are, that no flesh should glory in His presence. But of Him you are in Christ Jesus, who became for us wisdom from God—and righteousness and sanctification and

> redemption—that, as it is written, "He who glories, let him glory in the Lord."
>
> 1 Corinthians 1:26–31

God can and does use anyone He chooses for His glory. However, those whom He has transformed with a new spiritual nature—rich or poor, black or white, young or old, male or female—are far more sensitive and responsive to His prompting, walking in alignment with His perfect will, to be fully revealed in the Last Day:

> After these things I looked, and behold, a great multitude which no one could number, of all nations, tribes, peoples, and tongues, standing before the throne and before the Lamb, clothed with white robes, with palm branches in their hands, and crying out with a loud voice, saying, "Salvation *belongs* to our God who sits on the throne, and to the Lamb!"
>
> Revelation 7:9–10

My expectations have not diminished over the years. His grace and mercy continue to astound me, and His Word unfailingly affirms His goodness and faithfulness. I do not know what my immediate future holds, but I know the Lord holds it in His sovereign hands—*and I trust Him!*

One day, I, too, will finish this race when the Lord calls me home to be in the company of all those who have gone before me. Still, my Christian experience is very precious to me and is beautifully captured in this wonderful hymn I learned as a youth:

I Heard the Voice of Jesus Say
Horatius Bonar[5]

I heard the voice of Jesus say, "Come unto Me, and rest; Lay down, thou weary one, lay down Thy head upon My breast." I came to Jesus as I was, Weary and worn and sad; I found in Him a resting place, And He has made me glad.

I heard the voice of Jesus say, "Behold, I freely give The living water thirsty one, Stoop down, and drink, and live." I came to Jesus, and I drank of that life-giving stream; My thirst was quenched, my soul revived, And now I live in Him.

I heard the voice of Jesus say, "I am this dark world's Light; Look unto Me, thy morn shall rise, And all thy day be bright." I looked to Jesus, and I found In Him my Star, my Sun; And in that Light of life I'll walk Till trav'ling days are done.

There I will be with our blessed Lord, forever changed—to reflect His glory. Hallelujah!

What a Wonderful Savior!

Our life is one of great expectation as we stay rooted in God's Word, rely on His Spirit, pray, and fellowship with other believers regularly.

Over time, we grow to reflect Christ in our daily actions, choices, and relationships. We demonstrate our unwavering faith through love, humility, and a Christ-like life. We do this regardless of the circumstances we face. We grow to become living testimonies of God's miraculous power, drawing others to the hope, peace, and change found only in Jesus Christ:

> Let your light so shine before men, that they may see your good works and glorify your Father in heaven. Matthew 5:16

As new creatures in Christ, we persevere with God's power and perspective, even as we wait and prepare for our bright future. No longer spiritually dead, our new life craves the Lord and His righteousness.

We eagerly await our glorious final change with great expectation—earnestly desiring Christ and that wonderful day.

Notes

[1] William L. Lumpkin, "Articles of Faith Put Forth by the Baptist Bible Union of America," "section II, Of the True God," in *Baptist Confessions of Faith*, rev. ed. (Valley Forge, PA: Judson Press, 1969), 385.

[2] For a further discussion on God's sacred name (the Tetragrammaton), see J. Barton Payne, "484 הָוָה (hāwâ) II, the older form and rare synonym of hāyâ (q.v.), be, become," in *Theological Wordbook of the Old Testament*, vol. 1, ed. R. Laird Harris, Gleason L. Archer Jr., and Bruce K. Waltke (Chicago: Moody Press, 1981), 210–12; and W. E. Vine, Merrill F. Unger, and William White Jr., *Vine's Expository Dictionary of Biblical Words* (Nashville: Thomas Nelson, 1985), 140–41.

[3] Charles Hodge, "6. Eternity," sec. A, "A Scriptural Doctrine," in *Systematic Theology*, vol. 1, 3rd printing (Peabody, MA: Hendrickson Publishers, 2003), 385.

[4] "Born Again," "Second Birth," "In Christ," "New Birth," and "Union with Christ" describe aspects of the profound mysterious spiritual transformation that occurs when we encounter God. On the human side, conversion happens when we turn from sin in repentance and turn to Christ in faith. On God's side, regeneration happens as the Holy Spirit brings our dead spirits to life—He "quickens" us, making us new creatures in Christ. This union marks the beginning of our eternal salvation and abundant life that is Christ-centered and Holy Spirit-driven.

[5] Horatius Bonar, "I Heard the Voice of Jesus Say," in *The Baptist Standard Hymnal with Responsive Readings*, ed. Mrs. A. M. Townsend (Nashville: Townsend Press, 1961), 213.

Chapter Two

Chapter Two
Yearning for Christ and the Change He Brings

A Yearning for God

Yearning for God is a universal human experience. As we briefly covered earlier, in the Fall, we forfeited a perfect relationship with our Creator, leaving us with an inherent longing—a profound spiritual void.

Ours is not merely a desire for comfort but a yearning for communion—a return to the peace, love, and dignity to which our God created us.

Since the Fall, every human heart has experienced this void, often seeking to fill it with empty distractions like relationships, success, or possessions. All of these fail to satisfy our deepest spiritual hunger:

> For My people have committed two evils: They have forsaken Me, the fountain of living waters, and hewn themselves cisterns—broken cisterns that can hold no water.   Jeremiah 2:13

At its core, our yearning is for God. It is persistent; we cannot ignore or suppress it. This yearning is not passive; it calls us toward something greater than ourselves. It is an inner recognition that something vital has been lost and that only in Jesus Christ can we find the healing and peace we seek.

Ultimately, our yearning points us to the only One who can fulfill it. Through His sacrificial death on our behalf, Jesus offers the restoration we lost in the Fall, bridging the gap between our brokenness and God's wholeness.

In Him, we are transformed as God restores us to His original design—eternal, unbroken fellowship. Our yearning for Christ is not a human flaw, but God's invitation to abundant life, as He satisfies our souls, restores our brokenness, and makes us whole.

Our Need for a Radical Transformation
To grasp our need for a complete spiritual overhaul, consider the beginning, when God created a perfect world where we could fully experience His glorious presence.

In this idyllic setting, free from sin and death, we shared eternal bliss with Him, unencumbered in His loving unbroken fellowship.

God created us "in His image," distinct from all other creatures. He made us perfect as male and female to procreate and to exercise dominion as good stewards over His creation. (Genesis 1:27–28)

Our ancestors disobeyed God by eating from the Tree of the Knowledge of Good and Evil, defying His command. (Genesis 2:16–17) In that moment, we "fell" from perfection, and sin, decay, and death contaminated the entire world.

The most devastating outcome was our immediate separation from God—for as the Bible teaches:

> All have sinned and fall short of the glory of God.   Romans 3:23

We have a sin problem—a spiritual vacuum inside us that yearns to restore our pre-Fall intimacy with God, an intimacy that is unattainable through human efforts alone.

It is as if Adam and Eve's disobedience tilted the world forty-five degrees, and humanity has been sliding down its slippery slope ever since.

Although human kindness, technology, wealth, influence, and status can accomplish many things, they cannot reverse our downward trajectory.

When we perform good deeds, our sin-tainted nature skews our moral compass so that we still often fall short of God's standard of righteousness:

> There is a way that seems right to a man,
> but its end is the way of death.
>   Proverbs 14:12

We can never escape God's reckoning. Sin's price is death—eternal separation from God—because He is holy, and His response to sin is judgment. Yet, there is good news, as God says in Isaiah 45:22:

> Look to Me, and be saved, all you ends of the earth! For I am God, and there is no other.

God's Word also states:

> For the wages of sin *is* death, but the gift of God *is* eternal life in Christ Jesus our Lord. Romans 6:23

God did not leave us in our fallen condition. Through His gracious intervention, we can receive the precious, eternal fellowship we lost.

God's Intervention through Jesus Christ

Since our righteousness is inadequate, God Himself intervened through Jesus Christ, our perfect Mediator. He paid sin's price in full, filled the spiritual void, and restored our intimate fellowship with God. (Isaiah 53:4–6, Hebrews 9:11—15)

Old Testament prophecies foretold Jesus' miraculous birth, life, ministry, teachings, death, and resurrection with incredible detail and exactness:

- Genesis 12:3 foretells that, as Abraham's descendant, He would bless all nations.

- Isaiah 7:14 tells how a virgin will conceive and give birth to *Immanuel*, "God with us."

- Isaiah 53 details Jesus' crucifixion and suffering for sin, while Psalm 16:10 speaks of His resurrection.

The New Testament reveals Jesus Christ to be God in human flesh, unlike any other person who has ever lived—past, present, or future:

- His dominion over nature was evident as He turned water into wine, fed thousands with two fish and five loaves, walked on water, and He calmed a furious storm by His voice. (John 2:1–11, Matthew 14:13–21, Matthew 14:22–32, Mark 4:35–41)

- He proved to be the Great Physician when He healed a man with a withered hand, a lame man at Bethesda, the ten lepers, a woman with a bleeding disorder who touched His robe, and a certain blind man, whose healing and persecution is detailed in John 9. (Luke 6:6–11, John 5:1–15, Luke 17:11–19, Luke 8:43–48, John 9:1–38)

- He showed His dominion over death through the resurrection of Jairus' daughter, the Widow of Nain's son, Lazarus, and ultimately, Himself. (Luke 8:40–42, 49–56, Luke 7:11–17, John 11:1–44, John 20:14–20)

Our Christian faith is both unique and authoritative because it centers on the Lord Jesus Christ, who lived, died, rose from the dead, proclaimed, and proved to be the Son of God.[1]

His flawless yet simple teachings introduce a New Testament age, where forgiveness of sins and spiritual transformation are made possible by faith in Him.

Jesus Christ Our Mediator
In Him, we are free from the guilt, shame, and bondage of sin and death. Through His redemptive work, He restores our intimacy with God forever, just as He promises:

> Therefore if the Son makes you free, you shall be free indeed.   John 8:36

> Jesus said to him, "I am the way, the truth, and the life. No one comes to the Father except through Me."   John 14:6

The Lord is our Advocate before a holy and righteous God. He alone is our Intercessor whose atoning death secures our redemption forever:

> Therefore He is also able to save to the uttermost those who come to God through Him, since He always lives to make intercession for them.   Hebrews 7:25

No one has ever been, nor ever will be, His equal.

We Yearn for Christ
We yearn for the blessed change that only Jesus Christ can provide, confident that when we encounter Him personally, He transforms us forever.

By faith in Christ, God bestows eternal life upon us so that we can experience His perfect plan—our salvation:

> For God so loved the world that He gave His only begotten Son, that whoever believes in Him should not perish but have everlasting life. For God did not send His Son into the world to condemn the world, but that the world through Him might be saved. John 3:16–17

We yearn for Jesus Christ because our human endeavors do not invoke God's favor. Our righteousness is insufficient without faith in the Lord—His righteousness alone pleases God.

He is our hope, our peace, our expectation, and our glorious reward. As Galatians 3:11 reads, "The just shall live by faith," and 2 Corinthians 5:7 reminds us, "We walk by faith, not by sight." We look to Him, and we yearn for Him as our only Mediator.

After receiving Christ, our lives reflect the internal transformation of our thoughts and affections. This change is wrought by the Holy Spirit's regenerative work. We desire to emulate Christ's character and virtues, and to be with Him eternally.

Just as children instinctively rely on their parents, we look to Christ for our spiritual nourishment and care. We long for the sustenance He alone provides—spiritual food that strengthens us for growth and godliness. Through it, we learn to reflect our Lord's character and virtues:

> And Jesus increased in wisdom and stature, and in favor with God and men.
> Luke 2:52

Eternal Fellowship with Christ

The moment we enter into a relationship with Jesus Christ by accepting Him as Savior and Lord, He makes His permanent residence inside us as He promised:

> And I will pray the Father, and He will give you another Helper, that He may abide with you forever—the Spirit of truth, whom the world cannot receive, because it neither sees Him nor knows Him; but you know Him, for He dwells with you and will be in you.
> John 14:16–17

This Helper is the Holy Spirit, whom the Lord sends to indwell and guide us. Jesus also gives this personal invitation:

> Behold, I stand at the door and knock. If anyone hears My voice and opens the door, I will come in to him and dine with him, and he with Me.　　Revelation 3:20

Following our encounter with the Lord, many of us experience a burst of enthusiasm—an eagerness to follow Him, grow in intimacy, and serve as living witnesses of His grace and love.

> We love Him because He first loved us.
> 　　　　　　　　　　　　　1 John 4:19

At this stage, some of us will feel called to make radical life changes—embracing asceticism, withdrawing from worldly distractions, or pursuing a ministerial or monastic calling. Such efforts reflect our sincere attempts to forsake worldly concerns and fully dedicate our lives to serving the Lord.

Successfully Navigating My Initial Stage

In the early days of my Christian walk, I maintained personal devotionals, attended church regularly, nurtured family values, shared my faith, and served in various ministries. During this time, I pursued spiritual growth through discipleship at my local church and reached out to friends, classmates, and others with the gospel.

➢ A Nurturing Christian Family

As I shared earlier, God blessed me with a loving, nurturing Christian family. Mom, Dad, Grandma, and my two siblings valued and practiced a living, vibrant, authentic faith in Christ.

They expressed love for their children by not only telling us about the Lord Jesus Christ, but also by praying with us, reading the Bible together, and attending church every Sunday.

They were careful to instill Christian qualities and values that still resonate in me today. Their faith and fidelity helped cultivate my desire to know the amazing God they showed me consistently. Their actions spoke volumes!

I should also note that they were not just my parents and elders—they were also my friends, mentors, and exceptional spiritual examples.

Looking back, no one should ever trivialize the essential role that loving, nurturing, godly parents play in raising children in the right path—so that when they are older, they will not depart from it, as Proverbs 22:6 teaches. Two authors observe:

> There is no denying that culture and church play a major role in the developmental life of any person. But the role parents play in their children's lives far outweighs any other influence. What

parents believe and how they live out their beliefs (positively or negatively) has a huge impact on their children.[2]

In our fast-paced, modern society, we seldom consider applying the sound, biblical parenting I received as a child. With absentee parents, single-parent homes, and social media—along with popular opinion—taking on the role of raising children, it's no wonder so many children today are growing up with a very limited spiritual understanding.

While the culture of that day influenced my upbringing, I attribute the greatest part of my spiritual development to the combined efforts of three extraordinary people who introduced me to the Lord Jesus Christ and helped me understand how to live for Him daily.

Dad was the Chairman of the Deacons at our large metropolitan church, in addition to working full-time as a sanitation engineer. He also taught the adult men's Sunday school class, which I often attended and where I enjoyed watching him teach the Scriptures clearly and accurately.

Mom worked as a dietitian before she retired to become a full-time homemaker and caregiver for Grandma, my brothers, and me. She also taught children's Sunday school. When not overseeing us children at home, Grandma served faithfully in our church's food pantry and other outreach ministries at church.

Together, they encouraged and supported my spiritual growth by explaining fundamental biblical truths in ways I could understand and apply. Some authors observe:

> It's not enough to just provide materially for our children. It's the sole duty and highest responsibility for parents to cultivate spiritual truths in their children's lives as well.[3]

➢ A Solid Christian Church

My parents were not alone in my spiritual development. God placed us in a strong local church, led by a visionary pastor and a team of spiritually-mature leaders who prioritized sound Bible teaching and Christian discipleship.

Each week, I was immersed in sound biblical teaching and training through Sunday school, worship services, Laymen, the Training Union (or BTU), and mid-week prayer meetings. The church offered valuable ministry opportunities that nurtured both spiritual gifts and practical life skills through mentorship in areas like leadership, music, outreach, and support endeavors.

In addition, the Lord blessed us with astute Bible teachers who were adept at guiding students to grasp and integrate fundamental scriptural principles and doctrines essential to our spiritual growth and moral development.

These wonderful men and women became my extended family, providing the care, guidance, discipline, and counsel I needed to develop a vibrant Christian faith that resonates in me today.

In retrospect, I can see how God used them to spark a lifelong calling. That's why we must never underestimate the value of intentional, Bible-based discipleship for every age group. As one author puts it:

> So while effective Christian education isn't the only thing that matters in church life, it is by far the most influential factor in nourishing faith . . . congregations should be primarily about the task of "equipping saints" for ministry. The church structure and institution should empower people for ministry, rather than accomplishing the ministry for them.[4]

This author further observes:

> The challenge to congregations, then, is to help each member see himself or herself as an active minister—as a representative of Christ in the world. When local churches take seriously this responsibility to nurture each person's faith, the work of

the church will be done through and by its members, who are, after all, the church.[5]

The more I served in my church and community, the more passionate I became about serving Christ, especially when considering the prospects of eternal rewards:

> Do not lay up for yourselves treasures on earth, where moth and rust destroy and where thieves break in and steal; but lay up for yourselves treasures in heaven, where neither moth nor rust destroys and where thieves do not break in and steal. For where your treasure is, there your heart will be also.   Matthew 6:19–21

Although there were many unforgettable people who influenced me, these four in particular expanded the lessons my parents instilled in me.

> ➢ Four Very Important People

Music can deepen our connection with God by expressing profound emotions, reinforcing biblical truths, and fostering unity within the Body of Christ through psalms, hymns, and spiritual songs. (Ephesians 5:19, Colossians 3:16)

One music leader's inspiring ministry had a significant impact on me. His musical selections allowed me to recall Scriptures about God's majesty and splendor. As our congregation lifted our voices in worship, the melodies and lyrics helped me to focus on God while experiencing His reassuring presence and power in tangible ways.

Ultimately, my faith deepened and God was glorified. Those timeless songs and hymns remain a cherished and valuable part of my Christian experience to this day.

An office administrator also had a significant influence on my young life. He demonstrated the extraordinary ability to recite large portions of Scripture passages from memory, flawlessly. Each time he recited the Word in front of me—always with a broad smile, and warm chuckle—the Word seemed to come to life in my heart. Watching him motivated me to learn and recite the Word myself, which I eventually did.

Another spiritual giant in my young life was a compassionate pastor whose heart for people was undeniable as he spent countless hours listening to and helping those in need within his church and community. Even strangers felt welcome because of his infectious laugh and comforting presence.

Through him, I saw a reflection of the Good Shepherd, which inspired me to extend compassion to those I served—fellow church members, individuals at the rescue mission, and those in prison. After my ordination, I consistently sought to integrate that same compassionate, Christ-centered approach into every aspect of my ministry.

Years later, after I surrendered to God's call on my life to the ministry, there was another, more seasoned pastor, his face etched with the wisdom and grace of many decades of life and ministry experience, who kindly and graciously mentored me for several years.

He willingly shared from his vast knowledge to explain the importance of biblical interpretation (hermeneutics), sound Christian doctrine, ethical ministry, moral conduct, church governance, effective preaching (homiletics), and pastoral care.

In my many visits to his home, to his church study, and when I observed him during worship services, the air hung heavy with quiet contemplation as he spoke and I listened and learned how to model the tenets of 1 Timothy 4:16 (AKJV):

> Take heed unto thyself, and unto the doctrine; continue in them: for in doing this thou shalt both save thyself, and them that hear thee.

These and many other godly men and women inspired me with their solemn reverence for God and His Word, along with the fervor, anticipation, and vigilance of His imminent return.

No one is perfect, but I saw little hypocrisy. The more time I spent with them, listened to their personal faith stories, and observed their Christian conduct, the more they validated those wonderful faith stories for me. Nonetheless, these precious faith examples stirred in me a yearning, not just to grow closer to Christ, but also to serve Him the rest of my life.

➢ My Yearning to Grow and Serve

The rich spiritual foundation I received from my family and church ignited a personal desire to know the Lord for myself. The more I learned, the more I found their testimonies to be true—creating a life-long cycle of learning, experiencing, doing, and growing:

> But grow in the grace and knowledge of our Lord and Savior Jesus Christ. To Him *be* the glory both now and forever. Amen.
> 2 Peter 3:18

As I matured, I started teaching and helping others learn the principles my parents and others had taught me. I yearned to be approved by God in my handling of the Word:

> Be diligent to present yourself approved to God, a worker who does not need to be ashamed, rightly dividing the word of truth. 2 Timothy 2:15

After high school, I attended and graduated from a Bible college and later, seminary. After becoming an ordained minister, most of my adult life, I've served in churches around the country as a pastor, teacher, and ministry leader.

Even before college, I was actively involved in Christian service. I joined my church's evangelism team, where I regularly shared my faith. I later became engaged in ministry at the local rescue mission and then began visiting jails and prisons through our church's prison ministry team.

Prison ministry would eventually consume much of my bi-vocational life. Over the years, I served as a volunteer, program director, drug counselor, and institutional chaplain—roles I held as my family and I moved around the United States.

Throughout my preparation, I had the benefit of my parents' insight, along with godly, biblically-sound mentors who poured into me their wealth of knowledge, spiritual depth, and life experience. These influences helped me navigate the nuances of both the Christian faith journey and the ministry.

Yet, my most significant ministry roles have always been—as they still are—those of husband, father, and grandfather. These roles have brought me the most joy and fulfillment.

Yet, as my walk with Christ deepened, so too did my yearning for godliness in Christ.

Yearning for Godliness in Christ

Now that we are in Christ, the Holy Spirit lives within us to comfort us and influence our thoughts, words, and actions to emulate those of Jesus Christ. He also brings a renewed mind, which produces a growing distaste for worldly things while deepening our yearning for Christ and things that please Him:

> I beseech you therefore, brethren, by the mercies of God, that you present your bodies a living sacrifice, holy, acceptable to God, *which is* your reasonable service. And do not be conformed to this world, but be transformed by the renewing of your mind, that you may prove what *is* that good and acceptable and perfect will of God. Romans 12:1–2

God is a life-changing Holy Spirit whose majesty and splendor compel us to revere Him. Our godliness reveals His Spirit's work in us. Much like a compass needle signifies northern magnetic forces, our godliness points to God's Spirit, who is actively working in us.

Godliness is intentional, as we devote ourselves to things that help us grow closer to the Lord. We live with purpose by practicing things that please God with faith and spiritual due diligence. We explore our spiritual fruit, gifts, and armor under the guidance of pastors and mature spiritual advisors in a church setting through Christian discipleship.

We develop a craving for deeper intimacy with the Lord. We begin to invite Him to reign in every area of our lives, trusting Him to reveal His glory through us. God commands us to be holy, as He is holy. (Leviticus 20:26, 1 Peter 1:15–16)

We crave the sincere milk of the Word of God that we may grow thereby. (1 Peter 2:2) The Holy Spirit leads us on this journey of spiritual maturity through prayer, personal devotions, corporate worship, church participation, evangelism, and service to others.

Through these spiritual disciplines, we grow into Christlikeness with a yearning that moves us toward a lifelong process of sanctification, where the Holy Spirit continues His transforming work in us.

Achieving Godliness through Sanctification

As we pursue sanctification, the Holy Spirit helps us to outgrow our destructive tendencies toward sin, self, and Satan that can hinder our spiritual growth and nullify our Christian witness:

> We believe the Scriptures teach that sanctification is the process by which, according to the will of God, we are made partakers of his holiness; that it is a progressive work; that it is begun in regeneration; that it is carried on in the hearts of believers by the presence and

power of the Holy Spirit, the Sealer and Comforter, in the continual use of the appointed means—especially the word of God—self-examination, self-denial, watchfulness, and prayer; and in the practice of all godly exercise and duties.[6]

In our spiritual awakening, the Holy Spirit instills within us a desire to please God. Our sanctification is not a compulsory obligation, but a heartfelt response of gratitude for the transformed life God has freely given us.

As we experience His grace and discover His purpose for our lives, our excitement turns to fruitful action. We become not just hearers, but doers of God's Word:

> But be doers of the word, and not hearers only, deceiving yourselves. James 1:22

Sanctification leads us to visible change, so that others may see Christ in us. Our newfound life objective is to yield to the Holy Spirit's influence so we can grow in our faith and understand God's will for our lives. Then we can fully realize our identity as new creatures in Christ.

New Creatures in Christ

As new creatures in Christ, we demonstrate a new orientation, competence, and resources. The Holy Spirit gives us the confidence and purpose to navigate our Christian journey.

A New Creature Orientation

As we yield to the Holy Spirit's guidance, we choose God's will to be done in our lives. His fruit, the Fruit of the Spirit, becomes increasingly evident as we grow in Him spiritually:

> But the fruit of the Spirit is love, joy, peace, longsuffering, kindness, goodness, faithfulness, gentleness, self-control. Against such there is no law.
> Galatians 5:22–23

We serve as the Lord's hands and feet to extend His glorious presence to a world in need. Through His Spirit, we join Him in this mission—making godly, Spirit-led choices with purpose and resolve. The Fruit of the Holy Spirit is God's transformative blessing in our lives. As Galatians 5:16 teaches, when we walk in the Spirit, we do not fulfill the lusts of the flesh.

We cannot produce the Fruit of the Holy Spirit in our own strength. The Holy Spirit produces them as we live in harmony with God's purpose and plan as His noble ambassadors.

When we express the fruit—with love as the foundation of all the rest—we reflect God's grace and serve others in ways that transcend social barriers and personal expectations.

Let us take a closer look at how the fruit can shape our character, deepen our faith, and strengthen our relationships.

The Fruit of the Spirit
The Fruit of the Holy Spirit help us to display God's grace and compassion to an ever-observing world, with *love* at our core. Love is the supreme virtue. It is selfless, unconditional, and sacrificial—rooted in God's very nature. The Holy Spirit empowers us to love beyond our own capacity, extending selfless benevolence and grace regardless of a person's background, color, religion, or status. This love goes beyond feeling; it is action rooted in conscious choice and commitment. The Holy Spirit's influence on our transformed hearts makes this selfless love possible. Jesus taught that this love would be the defining mark of His followers before a watching, unbelieving world:

> By this all will know that you are My disciples, if you have love for one another.
> John 13:35

Our *joy* is the deep, abiding delight we have in our complete, fulfilling union with the Good Shepherd. It is reflected in a contentment and inner happiness that are unfazed by external events—rooted in our restored fellowship with God and the eternal hope that only He can give:

> Rejoice in the Lord always. Again I will say, rejoice! Philippians 4:4

Peace is the Spirit's work of internal calm and harmony. It arises from trusting in the Lord's sovereign control, producing a lasting sense of calm in our lives and surroundings. Because the Prince of Peace is with us, we can boldly face life's challenges and extend peace to others. Peace calms our anxieties, as we trust in God's sovereignty while He comforts, strengthens, and deepens our faith in Christ:

> And the peace of God, which surpasses all understanding, will guard your hearts and minds through Christ Jesus. Philippians 4:7

Longsuffering is our capacity to withstand long periods of discomfort, frustrating delays, or crushing disappointments without vengeful retaliation. It reflects God's patience with us and strengthens our relationships as we bear with one another in love. With compassion and empathy, we show patience and understanding in our interactions and commitments:

> With all lowliness and gentleness, with longsuffering, bearing with one another in love. Ephesians 4:2

We show **gentleness** –*also known as* **meekness**—in our civility. It is not weakness but strength under control, manifested in our humility and respect for others. Without pride or harshness, we create an atmosphere of empathy and understanding. Not demanding our own way, we respond with grace, listening intently, reflecting the heart of Jesus, who calls us to the same spirit:

> Blessed are the meek, for they shall inherit the earth.   Matthew 5:5

Goodness involves consistently performing noble acts, outwardly reflecting our spiritual transformation that points others to Christ. It manifests itself in noble acts of moral integrity, kindness, and generosity. Goodness always considers the well-being of others and is seen in our choices to "do the right things" that shape our faith and character, especially when no one is watching. The Holy Spirit empowers us to be honest and upright, guiding our actions from a renewed, pure heart. We operate with clarity and conviction because we want to please God:

> Do not be overcome by evil, but overcome evil with good.   Romans 12:21

Faithfulness means keeping our promises and commitments, even when difficulties arise or our initial enthusiasm wanes. Our dependability and trustworthiness mirror Christ's unwavering commitment, building trust and providing a sense of reliability for others. Faithfulness means more than just spoken promises. It is demonstrated through consistent, reliable actions that reflect Christ-like character:

> Moreover it is required in stewards that one be found faithful.   1 Corinthians 4:2

Kindness is a humble submission to God's will, much like our Lord's example. It begins with recognizing the dignity in every person and responds with grace, compassion, and empathy, even in the most challenging situations. Kindness gives freely—a selfless act without expectation of compensation. Kindness sees all humans as deserving compassion and builds bridges where division once stood, fostering peace, and reconciliation. Extending compassion creates a ripple effect, blessing others and our own lives:

> And be kind to one another, tenderhearted, forgiving one another, even as God in Christ forgave you.
> Ephesians 4:32

Self-control is the Holy Spirit's power in us to help us control our thoughts, words, and actions. It aligns our lives with God's Word and will, especially in moments of temptation or emotional impulse. Self-control is the key to living a disciplined and purposeful life by making choices that reflect Christ, rather than being controlled by impulse. The more we practice self-control, the more we experience the peace that comes from living in alignment with God's perfect will for our lives:

> But also for this very reason, giving all diligence, add to your faith virtue, to virtue knowledge, to knowledge self-control, to self-control perseverance, to perseverance godliness. . . . For if these things are yours and abound, *you* will be neither barren nor unfruitful in the knowledge of our Lord Jesus Christ.
> 2 Peter 1:5–6, 8

Together, these nine characteristics form a life that reflects the nature of Christ. As we experience these fruits more deeply in our own lives, we find ourselves more equipped to navigate life with grace, strength, and love. Each fruit is a blessing that not only transforms us but also blesses those around us. Through the Fruit of the Spirit, we become more like Christ, fulfilling our true purpose and bringing glory to God. The Holy Spirit not only transforms our character but He also equips us for service and spiritual battle.

A New Creature Competence
Not only does God endow us with His fruit, He also supplies us with effectual spiritual gifts to perform His work. These are not natural talents or acquired skills, but divine empowerments distributed for the purpose of serving others and building up the Church—the Body of Christ.

Spiritual gifts are vital because they are God's chosen means of accomplishing His will through His people. We use them to glorify Christ and advance His Kingdom, revealing His power, grace, and love—not for self-promotion:

> But one and the same Spirit works all these things, distributing to each one individually as He wills.
> 1 Corinthians 12:11

Eight Spiritual Gifts

The Holy Spirit distributes a variety of gifts throughout the body of Christ. Among them, these eight stand out as expressions of His power and grace.

Helpers (1 Corinthians 12:28) possess the Spirit-empowered ability to selflessly assist others in times of need. They are often first to respond when a need arises, and they prefer to serve quietly and avoid recognition. Their satisfaction comes from helping people, because they know God will reward their efforts. The Old Testament story of Ruth, who remained faithful to Naomi, is a fine biblical example of this gift.

Givers (Proverbs 3:27, Romans 12:8, Galatians 6:10), like helpers, cheerfully share their time, talents, and resources to meet others' needs. Responding quickly, and preferring anonymity, givers understand that God has entrusted them with resources not just for themselves, but also for the benefit of others. For them, it is more blessed to give than to receive. (Acts 20:35) Jesus' parable of the Good Samaritan is a great illustration of how givers act out of compassion and without concern for reward.

Wisdom (1 Corinthians 12:8, James 1:5) is the ability to perceive situations from God's perspective and offer clear, practical solutions rooted in truth. Those gifted with wisdom demonstrate more than intelligence; they express God-given insight. Solomon's wise decision between the two contesting mothers astonished all who witnessed it.

Exhorters (Romans 12:8) are encouragers who skillfully apply Scripture to uplift and strengthen other believers. They "come alongside others," inspiring hope and perseverance—especially in times of discouragement and doubt. Jonathan and Abigail, who exhorted David during his time of exile, are wonderful Old Testament examples.

Evangelists (Ephesians 4:11) have the unique ability to communicate the gospel in ways that compel others to respond in faith. While all believers are called to share their faith, the Holy Spirit empowers evangelists to do so with clarity and power—leading others to trust in Jesus Christ as their Savior and Lord. Philip, the evangelist, at Caesarea (Acts 21:8) is a solid New Testament example.

Pastors (Jeremiah 3:15, Acts 20:28, Ephesians 4:11, 1 Timothy 3:1–7, Titus 1:5–16) are the *under-shepherds* serving under the authority of Jesus Christ—the Good Shepherd—entrusted with the spiritual, moral, and practical well-being of the local congregation. As spiritually mature leaders, the Holy Spirit gifts them to provide ongoing spiritual care, guidance, and instruction to the local church. Their primary role is to shepherd believers toward spiritual and moral maturity in Christ. In fulfilling this calling, pastors offer biblical teaching, pastoral care, oversight, and encouragement, while also attending to the needs of the flock, just as Christ cares for us.

Teachers (Romans 12:7, Ephesians 4:11) are spiritually gifted to explain complex Scripture passages so that others can understand and apply its principles to life. They are passionate about preparing, analyzing, and presenting lessons in a way that is clear, relevant, and transformative, enabling students to deeply understand and effectively apply God's Word in their daily lives. The teacher's influence is enduring and central to discipleship, guiding others to understand God's purpose and instruction for their lives. Jesus' teaching was profoundly effective and transformative.

Leaders (Romans 12:8, 1 Corinthians 12:28) have the extraordinary gift of administration, with the ability to attract, capture, persuade, and lead others harmoniously, with tact and prudence. They cast vision, manage resources, and inspire others toward collective goals. They steward with integrity and wisdom, applying biblical principles to guide their decisions, while excelling in group dynamics, communication, and organizational management. One fine example is how God used Moses to lead the Children of Israel out of Egypt and through the wilderness.[7]

In my own Christian journey, I discovered very early that the Lord had given me a passion for exhortation, teaching, and leadership. Over time, He opened doors for me to use gifts—for His glory—I never would have imagined.

New Creature Resources
In a world of constant spiritual battle, God does not leave His children defenseless. He not only gives us spiritual fruit and gifts, He also equips us with His divine resources—the Armor of God—our personalized spiritual protection. Our armor enables us to stand firm against the enemy's schemes and walk in victory, not defeat.

The Armor of God
In the same way that soldiers wear body armor as physical defense, Christians are exhorted to wear spiritual armor to resist the attacks of Satan and live victoriously in Christ:

Finally, my brethren, be strong in the Lord and in the power of His might. Put on the whole armor of God, that you may be able to stand against the wiles of the devil. For we do not wrestle against flesh and blood, but against principalities, against powers, against the rulers of the darkness of this age, against spiritual *hosts* of wickedness in the heavenly *places.* Therefore take up the whole armor of God, that you may be able to withstand in the evil day, and having done all, to stand. Stand therefore, having girded your waist with truth, having put on the breastplate of righteousness, and having shod your feet with the preparation of the gospel of peace; above all, taking the shield of faith with which you will be able to quench all the fiery darts of the wicked one. And take the helmet of salvation, and the sword of the Spirit, which is the word of God; praying always with all prayer and supplication in the Spirit, being watchful to this end with all perseverance and supplication for all the saints.

Ephesians 6:10–18

More than symbolic, our armor plays a real and active role in our lives. Our fight is not to achieve victory, but to walk in the victory already won through Jesus' triumph over sin and death.

The *Girdle of Truth* is a foundational piece of armor that symbolizes God's truth, anchoring us in His Word and protecting our integrity. Truth shapes not only our beliefs but also our behavior. The girdle of truth calls us to live with integrity, honesty, and transparency, aligning our words and actions with God's truth. It helps ensure we do not live hypocritically or hide behind falsehoods. Just as a belt holds a soldier's armor together, God's truth holds everything in our spiritual life. The girdle of truth helps us recognize lies and stand firm in our faith.

The *Breastplate of Righteousness* guards our heart as we emulate the Lord's truth and integrity. It symbolizes our right standing with God, ensuring we live in alignment with His will, under the power of the Holy Spirit. God imputes righteousness to us, declaring us justified by faith in Jesus Christ—not by our works. (Romans 3:22–24; 5:1–2) The breastplate also symbolizes our righteous lifestyle—loving others, living justly, and avoiding sin—guarding us from temptation while standing firm in our faith.

The *Shoes of the Gospel of Peace (Shoes of Preparation)* provides the stable footwear we need for spiritual traction. The peace of God grounds us, gives us confidence, and prepares us to move forward with the Good News at God's urging. Our diligent study and preparation allow us to share biblical truths that benefit others and ourselves. (Psalm 119:105, 2 Timothy 2:15) Our stability and direction enable us to stand firm in our faith.

Our *Shield of Faith* protects us from spiritual assaults like doubt, fear, and temptation, just as a physical shield defends against attack. It blocks the fiery darts of the Enemy, helping us overcome life's challenges that test our faith. It gives substance to what we hope for and proves what we cannot see. (Hebrews 11:1) Ultimately, faith gives us access to remarkable power, even when the outcome remains uncertain.

Our *Helmet of Salvation* protects the head, a critical component of the body, preserving our minds within. This represents our salvation and the steadfast confidence we hold in the promise of eternal life and our security, grounded in our faith in the perfect work of Jesus Christ. As a soldier's helmet protects his head, the helmet of salvation protects our thoughts, identity, and focus. It guards us against doubt, fear, and deception. The assurance of our salvation in Christ brings us hope and freedom. Without spiritual rebirth, true effectiveness in Christ is impossible. We cannot guide others where we have not been or share knowledge we do not have. Jesus warns we risk leading others astray spiritually, like the "blind leading the blind." (Matthew 15:14) The Seven Sons of Sceva discovered this when they confronted an evil spirit that left them battered, bruised, and naked. (Acts 19:16)

Our *Sword of the Spirit* or the *Word of God* is a powerful and reliable weapon in spiritual warfare. It exposes lies, develops our faith, and leads us to the truth. With Scripture, we are able to resist deception, confront temptation, and follow God's direction. God's Word never fails—it accomplishes His will and fulfills His purpose wherever it is sent. (Isaiah 55:11) Just as Jesus overcame Satan in the wilderness by declaring, "It is written" (Matthew 4:1–11), we, too, overcome by standing firmly on the unchanging truth of God's Word.

Jesus encourages us to *pray*, and not to lose heart. (Luke 18:1) Prayer keeps us connected to our Lord and invites Him to intervene in every battle we face. The Holy Spirit guides us to pray without ceasing. (1 Thessalonians 5:17) In our most urgent moments, the Holy Spirit awakens longings deeper than words. In those moments, the Holy Spirit intercedes on our behalf. (Romans 8:26) Through prayer, we stay connected to our Lord, obtain strength, and intercede for others. We pray in Jesus' name, under His authority, as He instructed us. (John 14:13–14)

God is calling us to put on the whole armor of God, to stand firm, and to advance His Kingdom with courage and faith daily. We cultivate our desire for change and longing for Christ through prayer, worship, reflecting on His promises in Scripture, and maintaining an eternal perspective with Him as the center of our lives. Our desire grows as we turn our hearts away from the values of the world and fix our eyes on Jesus as "the author and finisher of our faith." (Hebrews 12:2) We long for change in the present by seeking to grow in our Christlikeness and fully experience the work of the Holy Spirit in our lives as the Bible teaches:

> If then you were raised with Christ, seek those things which are above, where Christ is, sitting at the right hand of God. Set your mind on things above, not on things on the earth. For you died, and your life is hidden with Christ in God. When Christ *who is* our life appears, then you also will appear with Him in glory.
> Colossians 3:1–4

We long for Christ's likeness to be formed in us now, through the transforming work of the Holy Spirit. Nevertheless, we also long for the day when all things will be made new—when Christ returns and we dwell with Him forever:

> For our citizenship is in heaven, from which we also eagerly wait for the Savior, the Lord Jesus Christ, who will transform our lowly body that it may be conformed to His glorious body, according to the working by which He is able even to subdue all things to Himself.
> Philippians 3:20–21

This dual longing, one for transformation in the present, and one for glorification in the future, shapes how we live today. It gives us strength to persevere through trials and faith to endure hardships with eternal hope for the future. Until that day, we walk by faith, growing in grace, and wait with eager anticipation.

Notes

[1] See Norman L. Geisler, "The Deity and Authority of Jesus Christ," in *Christian Apologetics*, 5th printing (Grand Rapids, MI: Baker Book House, 1991), 329–352; and Josh McDowell, "Resurrection—Hoax or History," in *Evidence That Demands a Verdict*, vol. 1, rev. ed., 29th printing (San Bernardino, CA: Here's Life Publishers, 1988), 179–263.

[2] Alex McFarland and Jason Jimenez, *Abandoned Faith: Why Millennials Are Walking Away and How You Can Lead Them Home* (Carol Stream, IL: Tyndale House, 2017), 31.

[3] *Ibid.*, 226.

[4] Eugene C. Roehlkepartain, *The Teaching Church: Moving Christian Education to Center Stage* (Nashville, TN: Abingdon Press, 1993), 26.

[5] *Ibid.*, 27.

[6] Edward T. Hiscox, *The Standard Manual for Baptist Churches*, "X. Sanctification" (Philadelphia, PA: Judson Press, 1951), 66.

[7] God endows non-clergy with teaching and leadership gifts also.

Chapter Three

Chapter Three
Waiting on God's Appointed Time for Change

Poised to Achieve the Dream
Waiting is how our Christian life truly takes shape. All that has happened before has prepared us for this moment—a daily yearning to be with the Lord, as Scripture reminds us:

> Not only *that,* but we also who have the firstfruits of the Spirit, even we ourselves groan within ourselves, eagerly waiting for the adoption, the redemption of our body. Romans 8:23

Yet we have tasks to perform—God is never finished with us, or with me. This is where my personal story continues.

The 1960s rang with voices that shaped a nation in turmoil. We witnessed historical, social, and political shifts: the Space Race, the Vietnam War, Civil Rights marches, the Black Panthers, counterculture movements, Berkeley protests, Woodstock, and Haight-Ashbury.

Music and pop culture stirred our hearts and shaped our identity—Motown, James Brown, Jimi Hendrix, Janis Joplin, The Beatles, The Beach Boys. Even our spiritual explorations found a voice in songs like "My Sweet Lord," "Day by Day," "O Happy Day," and "Aquarius / Let the Sunshine In."

Our hopes and frustrations were echoed in rallying cries and iconic slogans: "We Shall Overcome," "What the World Needs Now Is Love," "Say It Loud," "Burn, baby, burn," "Turn on, tune in, drop out"—while the troubling declaration "God is dead" echoed louder than many of our hearts could bear.

It was an era of sound and fury—rallies, riots, music, and mourning. The deaths of so many of our heroes—JFK, Malcolm, Martin, Bobby—forever shattered our nation's soul with sorrow.

Some of my contemporaries heeded destructive voices and chose paths that led to oblivion, while others embraced promising career opportunities and have made significant imprints in our world today.

Yet somewhere in the middle of all that turmoil stood one Black kid from the inner city—watching, listening, and learning.

As our leaders spoke of a new day, it stirred our hopes for a better tomorrow, with access to opportunities and resources previously unavailable to us.

Our astronauts landed on the moon, the '60s were behind us, and the '70s became our long-awaited moment to *realize "the Dream"* [1] and to embark on a brave new world. Nothing would be impossible!

However, as Psalm 118:8–9 warns, it is far better to place our confidence in the Lord than in fallible humans, no matter how well-meaning they may be:

> *It is* better to trust in the LORD Than to put confidence in man. *It is* better to trust in the LORD Than to put confidence in princes.

It soon became clear that no earthly leader or movement was worthy of ultimate trust. The years that followed were marred by a wave of high-profile moral failures, political opportunism, broken promises, and the rise of drugs, gangs, violence, trafficking, and exploitation—painting a grim picture of our hopes for a brighter day.

Fast forward to 2025, and we seem to be reliving our past hopes for a brave new world. However, certain truths have become abundantly clear in retrospect.

- Sin and its malevolent byproducts are inherent parts of our broken world. We will never achieve utopia (or heaven) on earth.

- Persuasive rhetoric will not compel love, especially when someone is deeply hurt or harboring bitterness or resentment toward the other person.

- No one can expect love or respect across racial lines without first having love and respect for themselves—and for their own race.

- Only Jesus Christ can transform even the worst of us into forgiven and free citizens of the Kingdom of God. Only through Him can we experience true and lasting peace, justice, dignity, and equality.

Many things have improved for those who took advantage of the opportunities that emerged in law, education, science, technology, and business.

We envisioned a society rooted in mutual respect, where our hard-won civil rights would usher in lasting harmony. Yet instead of gaining the understanding, common courtesy, and civility we had hoped for, we witnessed the opposite: a troubling rise in disrespect, hostility, and senseless violence—especially within our own communities—leaving many of us disillusioned.

We are free to express ourselves—appropriately, that is, without endangering the health, safety, or welfare of others. Civilized people are morally obligated to show consideration for their fellow citizens—regardless of color, class, or political affiliation.

We share a sacred duty to preserve public civility, decency, and goodwill, especially within our own families and communities. It is in our best interest to foster a congenial atmosphere. Otherwise, we will face more anarchy, aggression, and bloodshed, all of which jeopardize everyone's safety.

I am disturbed by what seems to be a growing racial hostility in the United States, where civility and understanding ought to prevail. I can recall the demonstrations, riots, and occupations that happened during my lifetime—in Birmingham and Selma, San Francisco, Berkeley, Watts, Newark, Washington, Cleveland, Chicago, Detroit, Kent State, Wounded Knee, and Alcatraz—that shaped our nation's social expression.

I am a natural-born U.S. citizen. The legacy of my foreparents—slavery, segregation, discrimination, and injustice—still evokes rage from many within my race even today. I, too, have had my share of unfortunate, racially-motivated events during my lifetime.

Some feelings of rage may seem to be justified, yet I have come to realize that ours is not a perfect world, and ours is not a perfect nation—no nation is. Exploitation and victimization happen everywhere around the globe, and no one race has "cornered the market" on being victimized. In this country alone, our history features other people— including Native Americans, Asians, Pacific Islanders, Irish, Italians, and Hispanics—who have also faced discrimination, injustice, and hostility.

Nevertheless, I am most grateful to the Lord for the opportunity to live in the United States of

America. He has blessed us with many opportunities, including the freedom to worship, to express our opinions without censorship, to elect our representation, and to travel where we want, when we want—freedoms we often take for granted. We also benefit from a capitalistic system that provides goods and services that enhance our standard of living and improve our overall quality of life—such that people around the world desire to become citizens and live here.

Yet these precious civic freedoms do not give us license to "do what we want when we want." Instead, our civic freedom means having the sacred responsibility to act in the best interest of our common good. That's why I am grateful for laws that guard against disorder when individual freedoms are taken to the extreme.

Our sin-nature guarantees that violence and injustice will persist as long as we live on earth. But as civil creatures created in the image of a holy God, we are called to exhibit a higher level of spiritual and moral acumen—one that accepts and embraces others so that we can enhance and preserve civil society. Otherwise, hostility and violence will continue to grow.

Let me also say that the spiritual darkness in our nation is deeply troubling. We seem to have forgotten that what truly makes a nation great is not its technology, politics, or military power, but its faith in God and commitment to Judeo-Christian values. As the Scriptures affirm,

"Righteousness exalts a nation, but sin is a reproach to any people." (Proverbs 14:34)

While no nation is perfect—ours included—we once had a clearer understanding of right and wrong. In our not-too-distant past, we instinctively upheld a moral standard, drawing a clear line of demarcation between what was good and what was not. Today, that line is increasingly blurred by sin and a growing sense of entitlement.

It became apparent that my destiny could never be found in any social or political system. I also understood that the "Dream" of Overcoming—of fulfilling the hopes and aspirations of both my generation and my parents'—had been reduced to simply "coming over" or embracing secularism as th e new normal. And this was not acceptable.

A Refocused "Dream"
The hollow allure of "just gettin' paid," adopted by many of my contemporaries, only deepened my conviction to continue the spiritual journey I had begun long before:

> Seek God and discover Him and make Him a power in your life. Without Him all of our efforts turn to ashes and our sunrises into darkest nights. Without Him, life is meaningless drama with the decisive scenes missing. But with Him we are able to rise from the fatigue of despair to the buoyancy of hope. With Him we are able to rise from the midnight of

desperation to the daybreak of joy. St. Augustine was right—we were made for God and we will be restless until we find rest in Him.²

Ultimately, the Lord calls us to something far more personal and spiritually gratifying:

> He has shown you, O man, what *is* good; And what does the LORD require of you But to do justly, To love mercy, And to walk humbly with your God?   Micah 6:8

Jesus Himself summarized it perfectly:

> "Therefore, whatever you want men to do to you, do also to them, for this is the Law and the Prophets."   Matthew 7:12

The tragic life stories of many of my contemporaries, which often led to bondage or death, were not for me. I did not want ungodly worldly influences to control my life.

The world's attempts to reduce my identity to just my skin color ultimately fail, because the Lord makes no race or class distinction:

> And He has made from one blood every nation of men to dwell on all the face of the earth, and has determined their pre-appointed times and the boundaries of their dwellings, so that they should seek the Lord, in the hope that they might

> grope for Him and find Him, though He is not far from each one of us.
>
> Acts 17:26–27

Instead, I wanted to experience the liberty and fullness I had heard about in sermons and read in Scripture.

Christ lives within me, and He sees all His children—including me—through His loving and affirming eyes. He uses all His children to work out His excellent, eternal plan, which far surpasses anything we could ever hope or imagine.

In John 16:33, the Lord tells us to take heart, for He has overcome the world. I realized that I had to trust Him completely, not my own understanding—acknowledging Him in every area of my life so that He could direct my path just as Proverbs 3:5–6 teaches.

He alone remains my confidence, especially in troubling and uncertain times. I understood that in Christ, I have an abundant life that would yield true success and ultimate victory forever:

> I can do all things through Christ who strengthens me.   Philippians 4:13

Primed for True Success and Victory

Although I was still very active in my church and maintained my personal devotions, around this time I felt a deep inner restlessness—as if God was calling me to something more.

I briefly worked as a social worker for an inner-city community agency and wrestled with several vocational paths. I considered becoming a full-time evangelist, traveling the country to share the Gospel of Jesus Christ. I also wondered if God might be calling me to serve as a missionary in a foreign country, sharing His love with others.

I struggled to discern God's will, and the uncertainty weighed heavily on me. After a season of fasting and prayer, I sought counsel from my family and pastors. Their wisdom and advice led me to leave home and enroll in a small Bible college. That pivotal decision would change the course of my life forever.

Ultimately, I would come to understand that I was primed for success and victory—not because of my own efforts, but because God made special provisions for me in this life. He guarantees our perseverance and victory through Christ, as one confession of faith affirms:

> We believe the Scriptures teach that such as are truly regenerate, being born of the Spirit, will not utterly fall away and perish, but will endure unto the end; that their persevering attachment to Christ is the grand mark that distinguishes them from superficial professors; that a special Providence watches over their welfare; and that they are kept by the power of God through faith unto salvation.[3]

God's Word also expresses this truth:

> The steps of a *good* man are ordered by the LORD, And He delights in his way. Though he fall, he shall not be utterly cast down; For the LORD upholds *him with* His hand. I have been young, and *now* am old; Yet I have not seen the righteous forsaken, Nor his descendants begging bread. Psalm 37:23–25

The pen the Lord uses to inscribe our names in the Lamb's Book of Life (Revelation 21:27) doesn't have an eraser. Our names are indelibly etched for eternity. God has chosen us, and He desires that we all experience His great love and forgiveness through Christ:

> The Lord is not slack concerning *His* promise, as some count slackness, but is longsuffering toward us, not willing that any should perish but that all should come to repentance. 2 Peter 3:9

Once we accept Christ and invite Him to reign and rule in our hearts as Lord and Savior, we no longer rely on our own strength to keep us. Instead, we rely on His strength to keep us—forever, as one writer observes:

> Since there is now an unchangeable and divine element in us, our salvation

depends no longer upon our unstable wills, but upon Christ's purpose and power. By temporary declension from duty, or by our causeless unbelief, we may banish Christ to the barest and most remote room of the soul's house; but he does not suffer us wholly to exclude him; and when we are willing to unbar the doors, he is still there, ready to fill the whole mansion with his light and love.[4]

We cannot keep ourselves, but our Almighty God can! The Psalmist writes:

> The Lord *is* your keeper; The Lord *is* your shade at your right hand. The sun shall not strike you by day, Nor the moon by night. The Lord shall preserve you from all evil; He shall preserve your soul. The Lord shall preserve your going out and your coming in From this time forth, and even forevermore.   Psalm 121:5–8

Someone once explained it to me this way: When we enter heaven, we pass under a great archway. On the front of it, we see a sign that reads, *"Whosoever will, let them come!"* However, once we are inside and look back, the same sign now reads, *"Welcome! The Elect from the foundation of the world!"*

From yearning to calling, from turmoil to trust—I had known the Lord personally for years. Now He was stirring in me an even stronger determination to live out my faith to share Christ with others, confident that He alone is my Guide and Keeper.

Occupy Until Jesus Comes

During my time at Bible college, the Lord led me to reflect deeply on two compelling themes. The first appears in Jesus' Parable of the Ten Pounds (or Minas), recorded in Luke's Gospel:

> He said therefore, A certain nobleman went into a far country to receive for himself a kingdom, and to return. And he called his ten servants, and delivered them ten pounds, and said unto them, Occupy till I come. Luke 19:12—13 (AKJV)

In this Parable of the Ten Pounds, when Jesus uses the term *"pound"* or *"mina,"* He refers to a unit of currency that represents about one hundred days' wages for the common worker.[5] While some sources have attempted to assign modern dollar equivalents, the key point is that each *mina* represented a substantial sum—emphasizing the value and responsibility entrusted to each servant.

In this illustration, all the servants were given approximately three months' wages, with the clear expectation to multiply it during the nobleman's absence. The application is that we are to produce fruit, because we are accountable for how we manage His entrusted resources.[6] Here is how Jesus describes that fateful encounter:

> Then another came, saying, "Master, here is your mina, which I have kept put away in a handkerchief. For I feared you, because you are an austere man. You collect what you did not deposit, and reap what you did not sow." And he said to him, "Out of your own mouth I will judge you, *you* wicked servant. You knew that I was an austere man, collecting what I did not deposit and reaping what I did not sow. Why then did you not put my money in the bank, that at my coming I might have collected it with interest?" And he said to those who stood by, "Take the mina from him, and give *it* to him who has ten minas." (But they said to him, "Master, he has ten minas.") "For I say to you, that to everyone who has will be given; and from him who does not have, even what he has will be taken away from him." Luke 19:20–26

God has given each of us a unique gift—something valuable to share with the world. All of us have something to offer the world. God enables us to leave a lasting impression on the lives of others around us. A person should never feel they have nothing to contribute—because they absolutely do.

Some are blessed with creative gifts such as painting, music, dance, or storytelling, while others are intellectually inclined, with strengths in critical thinking, problem solving, or teaching. Many have relational and emotional gifts like empathy, encouragement, and the ability to bring peace or offer wise counsel.

There are also spiritual and moral gifts—such as faith, leadership, discernment, and a heart for service—that inspire and uplift others. Practical abilities, like organization or financial stewardship, are just as vital and impactful. Ultimately, each gift becomes even more powerful when shaped by God's loving and caring hands.

God expects us to use our spiritual gifts, talents, and resources to further His divine plan. We are encouraged to remain diligent and not become complacent in any area of our Christian walk, for we are accountable for how we live:

> So then each of us shall give account of himself to God.   Romans 14:12

Under the Lord's power and authority, we can leverage our resources constructively and offer a faithful account of our actions when He returns.[7] One commentator explains it this way:

> The parable of the Pounds places visibly before our eyes not only the life-calling of the apostles, but also that of all believers. . . . As bond servants of their Lord they are

called to wait for His return, and that not inactive rest, but in zealous activity ... to proceed with their labor. In the humble position of witness to the faith, they must seek with word and deed to spread abroad God's kingdom, and expect their share in the government of the world, not before, but only after, the personal return of the Lord.[8]

In the King James Version of this parable, Jesus instructs us to "occupy till I come." The word "occupy" in this context is translated from the Greek word *pragmateuomai* (Strong's NT 4231), which means, "to do business," "to trade," or "to be engaged in enterprise." This term goes beyond mere busyness to convey the idea of being actively involved in meaningful work.

It suggests our due diligence, productivity, and faithful stewardship of the resources and responsibilities entrusted by the Lord. It also implies ongoing effort: to operate, to accomplish, to toil, and to conduct business with clear purpose.

Jesus emphasized how the equal portions He's given us are tools for testing our faithfulness, initiative, and capacity, which ultimately determine our readiness for greater kingdom opportunity:

> And so it was that when he returned, having received the kingdom, he then

commanded these servants, to whom he had given the money, to be called to him, that he might know how much every man had gained by trading. Then came the first, saying, "Master, your mina has earned ten minas." And he said to him, "Well *done,* good servant; because you were faithful in a very little, have authority over ten cities." And the second came, saying, "Master, your mina has earned five minas"' Likewise he said to him, "You also be over five cities."

Luke 19:15–19

The lesson calls us to look beyond material wealth and recognize the broader responsibility of faithful stewardship over all that God entrusts to us, as we await our eternal reward—even in a world that may be indifferent or hostile to Christ.

Luke 19:14 reveals that not everyone will acknowledge Jesus as Lord. Yet, we are still called to remain faithful stewards—even when society resists or rejects our values and mission.

The Lord calls us to live each day with purpose and commitment, wisely investing our time, talents, and resources until He returns or calls us home.[9]

Waiting with Purpose
Job 14:14 (AKJV) reads:

> All the days of my appointed time will I wait, till my change comes.

Job's waiting was not a passive resignation to his circumstances, but an active trust in God's timing through purposeful obedience. Similarly, our waiting is an active demonstration of faith in His imminent return, with a purposeful commitment to carry out His work until He comes.

Our waiting is wrapped in hope, secured by His triumphant death and resurrection. We are motivated by the hope of Christ's return, knowing that His kingdom will be fully established and every wrong will be made right:

> For to me, to live *is* Christ, and to die *is* gain. Philippians 1:21

We vigilantly wait in the tension between what Christ has already accomplished and what is yet to be fulfilled.

We live in a world that is already redeemed through His death and resurrection of Jesus, yet is still awaiting the full consummation of that redemption at His return.

As we wait, we are called to extend God's kingdom by letting Him work through us to influence the spiritual and moral climate around us.

Faithful waiting calls for us to be alert to God's work in our lives and in the world. We live with the awareness that Christ will return, and so we live for Him faithfully until that day.

Just as Job waited in faith, trusting in God's timing, so too are we called to wait with purpose, remaining vigilant with the hope of Christ's return.

As we wait for Christ to return, may we also watch with eyes wide open, living as faithful witnesses to His love and truth in a world that desperately needs both.

Our Earnest Expectation: A Perfecting Work
On one occasion, Jesus was displeased when His disciples rebuked those who brought children to Him for a blessing:

> But when Jesus saw *it*, He was greatly displeased and said to them, "Let the little children come to Me, and do not forbid them; for of such is the kingdom of God. Assuredly, I say to you, whoever does not receive the kingdom of God as a little child will by no means enter it." And He took them up in His arms, laid *His* hands on them, and blessed them.
> Mark 10:14–16

We seek the Lord with simple, child-like faith. He calls us His children, and like children on special occasions like birthdays and Christmas Eve, our waiting isn't idle; it's full of hope and activity as if something very special is about to happen.

The difference is our expectation has no definite timing, as it could be today, or one-thousand years from today. Yet, we wait with great anticipation for His glorious return.

While we are waiting, everyone starts at the same point—*Born Again*—as the Holy Spirit perfects these three virtues within us:

> ➤ *Loyalty (or Devotion)*

Loyalty is our deep commitment to confess and follow the Lord, regardless of the circumstances we face. It means surrendering to Christ while remaining devoted to Him—even when tested with difficulty, change, or temptation. We demonstrate loyalty by putting the Lord first in all our activities and commitments, and by being trustworthy—someone others can depend on; by showing consistency—remaining true to biblical principles even when it is inconvenient or costly, and especially by maintaining allegiance to our Christian faith—expressing a strong sense of belonging and duty to the Lord:

> Therefore whoever confesses Me before men, him I will also confess before My Father who is in heaven. But whoever denies Me before men, him I will also deny before My Father who is in heaven.
> Matthew 10:32–33

> *Willingness (Initiative)*

Willingness is the courage to take the first step in trusting God to use us for His glory. God entrusts every believer with resources—time, spiritual gifts, abilities, and influence. He expects us to act on our faith, not passively wait.

Willingness contrasts sharply with spiritual passivity, which is often masked as waiting on God, when it could actually be rooted in fear, doubt, or complacency. Where willingness says, "I trust God enough to obey Him now, even if I cannot see the outcome, passivity says, "When God makes everything clear, then I'll trust Him."

Initiative in the Kingdom of God means proactively using the resources we've been given for His purposes—trusting Him for the results and believing that He will reward our faithfulness. The Lord calls us to steward what we have, for His glory—right now—confident that our reward will come when Christ returns:

> Those who sow in tears Shall reap in joy. He who continually goes forth weeping, Bearing seed for sowing, Shall doubtless come again with rejoicing, Bringing his sheaves *with him.*   Psalm 126:5–6

> *Character (Integrity)*

Our character or integrity is the quality of being honest, upright, and consistent in our values and actions, especially when it's difficult or when no one is watching. It's a cornerstone of Christian character because it reflects the very nature of God—who is always faithful, just, true, and holy.

In a world that often rewards shortcuts, excuses, or pretense over substance, moral integrity stands out. For the Christian, it's a vital part of our witness and calling. Jesus doesn't just call us to believe—He calls us to live with honesty, dignity, and purpose.

When we walk in integrity, we reflect His character and demonstrate that we are faithful stewards of His grace before a watching world. Moral integrity is not defined by our perfection, but by sincerity of heart and our consistent courage to choose what is right. God does not expect flawless results—He knows our limitations all too well. He expects faithful and willing hearts:

> For their heart was not steadfast with Him, Nor were they faithful in His covenant. But He, *being* full of compassion, forgave *their* iniquity, And did not destroy *them.* Yes, many a time He turned His anger away, And did not stir up all His wrath; For He remembered that they *were but* flesh, A breath that passes away and does not come again. How often they provoked Him in the wilderness, *And* grieved Him in the desert!   Psalm 78:37–40

Even Jesus calls us beyond complacency:

> Therefore you shall be perfect, just as your Father in heaven is perfect. Matthew 5:48

His perfection is our maturity, wholeness, and love that reflect the heart of God. What matters most is our faithful response to God's call. He desires that we act with initiative, trust, and responsibility—not shrinking back in fear, but stepping forward in faith:

> But without faith *it is* impossible to please *Him,* for he who comes to God must believe that He is, and *that* He is a rewarder of those who diligently seek Him. Hebrews 11:6

Ultimately, the Lord's perfecting work in us raises two key questions: Will we be diligent workers in His Kingdom? And can we be trusted with the precious resources He has entrusted to us?

Vigilantly Watch for Jesus' Return
The second compelling theme appears in the New Testament passage concerning our readiness during the End Times recorded in Mark's Gospel:

> But of that day and *that* hour knoweth no man, no, not the angels which are in heaven, neither the Son, but the Father. Take ye heed, watch and pray: for ye know not when the time is. *For the Son of man is* as a man taking a far journey, who left his house, and gave authority to his servants, and to every man his work, and

commanded the porter to watch. Watch ye therefore: for ye know not when the master of the house cometh, at even, or at midnight, or at the cockcrowing, or in the morning: Lest coming suddenly he find you sleeping. And what I say unto you I say unto all, Watch.

Mark 13:32–37 (AKJV)

The Greek *grégoreó* (Strong's NT 1127), translates as "to watch," "to be vigilant," "to stay awake." It carries the sense of being awake and alert and suggests a kind of watchfulness that is proactive, not passive. It is about living with anticipation, ready for whatever might come, and prepared to act in accordance with God's will. We are admonished to watch and wait, to maintain our spiritual vigilance and readiness. This means to resist temptation and stay alert and prepared for the glorious return of Christ.[10]

In Mark 13, Jesus speaks of the end times, warning His disciples to be ready for His return. He describes the signs that will precede His coming, including tribulation, false messiahs, apostasy, and cosmic disturbances.

Yet, at the very end of this discourse, He gives them one clear command: *"Watch!"*

Jesus isn't merely warning about the future; He's calling for our present vigilance. The call to "watch" is a summons to spiritual alertness—to live in a state of readiness for His return, to recognize that the day of the Lord could come at any time. This watching is active. It involves living in anticipation, not just waiting idly but also living out the mission He gave His disciples: to proclaim and live out the Gospel message before the world.

In the same way that Job had to wait with active hope, Jesus calls us to wait with disciplined attentiveness as we guard not only our doctrine but also our decisions. We are to keep our spiritual eyes open, understanding that Christ's return is certain, even if the exact moment is unknown.

Jesus' call to watch also encompasses our spiritual lives, causing us to live with expectancy, ever alert to the signs of His coming. Watching creates a focused obedience, not just with eyes on the sky, but also with hearts focused on God's mission in the world today. The command to watch is not just a warning about the future; it is an urgent call to be spiritually vigilant in the present. One author puts it this way:

> The stiff wooden quality about our religious lives is a result of our lack of holy desire. Complacency is a deadly foe of all spiritual growth. Acute desire must be present or there will be no manifestation of Christ to His people. He waits to be wanted. Too bad that with many of us He waits so long, so very long, in vain.[11]

As we live in the now, aware of God's work in our world—through the signs of the times as revealed through Scripture—we live with an eternal perspective, aware of His coming kingdom.

Watching helps us not to become caught off guard by modern distractions—technology, social media, consumerism—and falsehoods that will come, as the world grows darker. It also helps us with discerning the times in which we live—in relation to the signs that Jesus described, which many feel are increasingly visible in today's world. Wars, persecution, false teachings, and global crises are all part of the environment in which we are called to remain alert.

Jesus tells us that although we live in the world, we are not of the world. (John 17:14) Our values, behaviors, and mindset should look different from the culture around us as one author notes:

> "In but not of" is our relationship "with" the world. Biblical Christians are to be "in" the world but not "of" the world. It pertains to our character—the kind of life we lead. We are aliens and strangers in the land, pilgrims passing through on our way to the Celestial City.[12]

On the other hand, Jesus' call to watch is a reminder that waiting doesn't mean being passive—staring upwards, completely mesmerized by some "pie-in-the-sky" fantasy. Living with spiritual awareness calls us to pay close attention to our daily lives, our choices, our actions, and our mission.

Staying Grounded and Focused

Over the years, two key Scripture passages have helped to keep me grounded and focused.

In His *Parable of the Sower*, Jesus spoke of a sower who spread seed by the wayside, on rocky soil, among thorns, and on good ground. Yet only the seed that fell on good ground produced fruit:

> But others fell on good ground, sprang up, and yielded a crop a hundredfold.
>
> Luke 8:8

The parable lesson is sobering: though many will hear the Gospel message, few will respond in a way that results in lasting transformation and fruit production. It is imperative for us who are serving to remain spiritually vigilant, attentive to how the Holy Spirit works in and through us. For in so doing, we guard how we produce fruit and multiply our harvest for our Lord.

In the *Parable of the Wise and Foolish Virgins* (Matthew 25:1–13) five were prepared to meet the bridegroom while the other five were not. When the bridegroom arrived, the five foolish virgins had gone to buy oil at the last minute and were too late to join the wedding party:

> And while they went to buy, the bridegroom came, and those who were

> ready went in with him to the wedding; and the door was shut.   Matthew 25:10

The lesson is to be ready always, not because we know the exact time of the Lord's return, but because, like the wise virgins, we choose to live in a constant state of spiritual readiness. Their watchfulness wasn't about predicting the moment—it was about being prepared when it came.

From reading Mark 13:37, the importance of being continually mindful of my conduct and surroundings became abundantly clear.

The passage reinforces the idea that Jesus is coming again—*literally*—and that at any moment I can expect Him to return "coming on the clouds of heaven with power and great glory." (Matthew 24:30) This begs the question: Will He find me faithful? What immediately follows His return, as presented in Matthew's Gospel, is even more sobering:

> And He will send His angels with a great sound of a trumpet, and they will gather together his elect from the four winds, from one end of heaven to the other.
> Matthew 24:31

I rely on the Lord's enduring strength to make a conscious and deliberate effort each day to refrain from speech and behavior that is detrimental to the cause of Christ or my Christian witness.

Because when I stand before the Lord on the "Last Day," I don't want to hear Him say:

> And then I will declare to them, 'I never knew you; depart from Me, you who practice lawlessness!' Matthew 7:23

Jesus offers the perfect illustration here:

> But if that evil servant says in his heart, 'My master is delaying his coming,' and begins to beat his fellow servants, and to eat and drink with the drunkards, the master of that servant will come on a day when he is not looking for him and at an hour that he is not aware of, and will cut him in two and appoint him his portion with the hypocrites. There shall be weeping and gnashing of teeth.
> Matthew 24:48–51

No one is perfect, and I have not had 100% success on every occasion. Regrettably, there were times when these infamous words were true in my case:

> For the good that I will *to do,* I do not do; but the evil I will not *to do,* that I practice.
> Romans 7:19

Yet, trusting the Lord to perform His work through me has been a tremendous blessing—to me—and to those I've had the opportunity to serve over the years.

In watching, we trust the Holy Spirit to help us maintain a godly perspective as we keep our eyes on Jesus, just as Scripture instructs:

> Therefore we also, since we are surrounded by so great a cloud of witnesses, let us lay aside every weight, and the sin which so easily ensnares *us,* and let us run with endurance the race that is set before us, looking unto Jesus, the author and finisher of *our* faith, who for the joy that was set before Him endured the cross, despising the shame, and has sat down at the right hand of the throne of God.   Hebrews 12:1–2

God's timing is always perfect. Therefore, waiting means living with open eyes and engaged hearts—trusting His timing and involving Him in our daily lives.

It also includes watching: living on mission, sharing the Gospel, and staying mindful of Whose we are—so that we remain faithful in the small things that advance God's Kingdom wherever we go so that whether we're at work, at school, in church, in the community, or at home, our aim is the same: to reflect the character of Christ.

Ultimately, our successful watching and waiting depends not upon us, but upon the Lord and His power to sustain us.

Notes

[1] "The Dream" refers to the vision of racial justice and equality articulated by Rev. Dr. Martin Luther King, Jr. in his *"I Have a Dream"* speech, delivered during the March on Washington for Jobs and Freedom, August 28, 1963.

[2] Coretta Scott King, *The Words of Martin Luther King, Jr.*, 1st. ed. (NY:NY: Newmarket Press, 1983) 64.

[3] Edward T. Hiscox, *The Standard Manual for Baptist Churches,* "XI Perseverance of Saints" (Philadelphia, PA: Judson Press, 1951), 67.

[4] Augustus Hopkins Strong, *Systematic Theology*, rev. ed., vol. 3, *The Doctrine of Salvation*, "Union with Christ: The Application of Christ's Redemption, in its Actual Beginning" (Philadelphia: Judson Press, 1976), 801.

[5] See Cecil B. Murphey, "Money, Minerals, and Gems," in *The Dictionary of Biblical Literacy*, ed. Lila Empson (Nashville: Oliver-Nelson Books, 1989), 342

[6] See Merrill F. Unger, "Metrology, 'Pound,'" in *Unger's Bible Dictionary*, 18th printing (Chicago: Moody Press, 1972), 720–726; James M. Freeman, "785, The 'Pound,'" in *Manners and Customs of the Bible*, reprint edition (Plainfield, NJ: Logos International, 1972), 420; Thomas R. Schreiner, "Luke" "IV. Galilee to Jerusalem: Discipleship (9:51—19:27)," in *Baker Commentary on the Bible*, ed. Walter A. Elwell, 5th printing (Grand Rapids, MI: Baker Books, 2008), 831–832.

[7] See "A. The Progress to Jerusalem. 18:31–19:27," in *The Gospel According to Luke*, in *The Wycliffe Bible Commentary*, ed. by Charles F. Pfeiffer and Everett F. Harrison (Chicago, IL: Moody Press, 1972), 1060.

⁸J. J. Van Oosterzee, "5. Jesus in Relation to the Sanguine Hopes of His Disciples (vv. 11–27)," in *The Gospel According to Luke*, vol. 8 of *Lange's Commentary on the Holy Scriptures: Matthew to Luke*, ed. John Peter Lange, trans. Philip Schaff and Charles C. Starbuck, 7th printing (Grand Rapids, MI: Zondervan Publishing House, 1980), 291–92.

⁹See 4231, πραγματεύομαι (*pragmateúomai*), in Spiros Zodhiates, *The Complete Word Study Dictionary: New Testament* (Chattanooga, TN: AMG Publishers, 1992), 1208; and Alexander Balmain Bruce, "Chapter XIX: Zacchaeus. Parable of the Pounds. Entry into Jerusalem," in *The Expositor's Greek Testament*, vol. 1, *The Synoptic Gospels*, ed. W. Robertson Nicoll (Grand Rapids, MI: Eerdmans Publishing Company, 1980), 605–6.

¹⁰See "1127. γρηγορέω (*grēgoreúō*)," in Spiros Zodhiates, *The Complete Word Study Dictionary: New Testament* (Chattanooga, TN: AMG Publishers, 1992), 384–85; "γρηγορέω," in *A Greek-English Lexicon of the New Testament and Other Early Christian Literature*, trans. and ed. William F. Arndt and F. Wilbur Gingrich, 2nd rev. ed., based on Walter Bauer's work (Chicago, IL: University of Chicago Press, 1979), 167; Alexander Balmain Bruce, "Vv. 32–37. Concluding Exhortation," in *The Expositor's Greek Testament*, vol. 1, *The Synoptic Gospels*, ed. W. Robertson Nicoll (Grand Rapids, MI: Eerdmans Publishing Company, 1980), 433.

¹¹A. W. Tozer, *The Pursuit of God: The Human Thirst for the Divine* (Camp Hill, PA: Wingspread Publishers, 2006), 17.

¹² Patrick M. Morley, *The Rest of Your Life* (Grand Rapids, MI: Zondervan Publishing House, 1998), 26.

Chapter Four

Chapter Four
Preparing for the Change God Has for Us

A Wonderful Change Awaits Us
To prepare for the change God has for us—a new heaven and new earth—we explore the subject of Eschatology, or "Last Things."

Many eschatological views share the belief that the new heaven and new earth will be the final state of the redeemed, where God will dwell with His people forever, and all things will be made new, as the Bible teaches.

However, the exact timing and nature of those events have been interpreted differently and debated across various systems of philosophical and religious thought:[1]

- Premillennialism: Affirms that Jesus Christ will return before a literal 1,000-year reign on earth. Those embracing the view of dispensationalism—the belief that God works in distinct periods (dispensations) of human history—typically align with this view.
- Amillennialism: Holds that there is no literal 1,000-year reign; the "Millennium" is symbolic of Christ's reign on earth—through His church. Early and modern Reformed thinkers have embraced the view that Christ is at work both in His people and through His church in our world now.

- Postmillennialism: States that the Lord will return after a period of Christian triumph and peace on the earth. Proponents of this view anticipate a time of worldwide Gospel influence, before Christ's return, brought about through the universal advancement of the Gospel message.
- Preterism: Interprets many prophetic passages, including those in Revelation, were fulfilled in the past—especially in the first century A.D. Many historical theologians view the events surrounding the fall of Jerusalem in 70 A.D. as fulfillments of these prophecies.
- Futurism: Maintains that our focus should be on future events with most biblical prophecies still to be fulfilled. Several dispensational thinkers align with this view. Some who hold a pre-tribulation rapture view have been widely popularized in modern culture along with a future fulfillment of Revelation's prophecies.
- Idealism: Sees prophecies as symbolic and allegorical, illustrating timeless spiritual truths. Theologians and scholars who hold this view argue that the symbolic messages found in Revelation as portraying the eternal conflict between good and evil, are applicable to every age—not just to those living in the "end times."

Nevertheless, Christians everywhere unite in our earnest expectation of our Lord's return, as this author observes:

No matter what their differences on the details, all Christians who take the Bible as their final authority agree that the final and ultimate result of Christ's return will be the judgement of unbelievers and the final reward of believers, and that believers will live with Christ in a new heaven and a new earth for all eternity. God the Father, Son, and Holy Spirit will reign and will be worshiped in a never-ending kingdom with no more sin or sorrow or suffering.[2]

Our day of change presents the ultimate transformation for Christians when Christ returns. Jesus paints this picture of our glorious expectation:

> When the Son of Man comes in His glory, and all the holy angels with Him, then He will sit on the throne of His glory. All the nations will be gathered before Him, and He will separate them one from another, as a shepherd divides *his* sheep from the goats. And He will set the sheep on His right hand, but the goats on the left. Then the King will say to those on His right hand, "Come, you blessed of My Father, inherit the kingdom prepared for you from the foundation of the world."
>
> Matthew 25:31–34

Jesus' compelling call invites us to be ready for eternity, for this will be the day of resurrection—the glorification of all believers everywhere, and the beginning of a world to come where human suffering ends forever:

> [We believe] That the end of the world is approaching; that at the last day Christ will descend from heaven, and raise the dead from the grave to final retribution; that a solemn separation will then take place; that the wicked will be adjudged to endless punishment, and the righteous to endless joy; and that this judgment will fix forever the final state of men in heaven or hell, on principles of righteousness.[3]

This is the ultimate fulfillment of God's promises to His children. We will be transformed into the image of Christ, receiving new, incorruptible bodies, and God shall wipe away all tears from our eyes, by removing death and sorrow forever.

Living with diligence now prepares us to meet Christ and share in His glory when the day of change arrives. Our diligence does not earn us the glorious future—it is entirely by God's grace that we are saved and transformed, just as our Lord taught us:

> "And which of you, having a servant plowing or tending sheep, will say to him when he has come in from the field,

'Come at once and sit down to eat?' But will he not rather say to him, 'Prepare something for my supper, and gird yourself and serve me till I have eaten and drunk, and afterward you will eat and drink?' Does he thank that servant because he did the things that were commanded him? I think not. So likewise you, when you have done all those things which you are commanded, say, 'We are unprofitable servants. We have done what was our duty to do.' " Luke 17:7–10

Yet, our faith compels us to prepare—to live holy lives, and to persevere as we await the fulfillment of God's promises. Each day, our lives should reflect the reality of our future hope, just as the Word declares:

Nevertheless we, according to His promise, look for new heavens and a new earth in which righteousness dwells. Therefore, beloved, looking forward to these things, be diligent to be found by Him in peace, without spot and blameless.
2 Peter 3:13–14

Our preparation is not burdensome but joyful, for we live today in the light of eternity, eagerly awaiting the world to come.

Five Things to Expect
Our day of change will be nothing short of glorious. While our final transformation is a gift of God's grace, we are called to live in joyful readiness, purifying ourselves and keeping our eyes fixed on the hope of eternity.

As we prepare, we can expect a Final Judgment resulting in a separation between the Righteous and the Wicked—by holding each person accountable for how they lived on earth.

Yet, we can expect these five things to occur on that grand and glorious day.

➤ *The Glorious Presence of the Lord*
The first thing we will experience is the glorious, radiant presence of our Creator—*in His fullness!* It will be a magnificent sight—one that defies all human description.

God's eternal presence will not be merely spiritual nearness but also a transforming reality. We will bask in the fullness of His glory and grace. It is the restoration of what was lost in the Garden of Eden and the culmination of His redemptive plan—a life where worship, purpose, and joy are forever found in the light of His resplendent face:

> But I saw no temple in it, for the Lord God Almighty and the Lamb are its temple. The city had no need of the sun or of the moon to shine in it, for the glory of God illuminated it. The Lamb *is* its light. And

the nations of those who are saved shall walk in its light, and the kings of the earth bring their glory and honor into it. Its gates shall not be shut at all by day (there shall be no night there). And they shall bring the glory and the honor of the nations into it. But there shall by no means enter it anything that defiles, or causes an abomination or a lie, but only those who are written in the Lamb's Book of Life.
Revelation 21:22–27

To be in God's presence forever means to live in an eternal, perfect relationship with Him—free from sin, pain, and death. It is the fulfillment of our deepest longing: to dwell with God in perfect peace and joy.

In Exodus 33:18–34:8, Moses longed to see God's glory at Sinai, but God warned him that no human could look upon His face and live. God sheltered Moses in a cleft of the rock and passed by, allowing him to see only His back.

Moses' brief glimpse of God's back caused his face to shine so brightly that he had to wear a veil to avoid alarming the people when he spoke to them. (Exodus 34:29–35, 2 Corinthians 3:12–18)

Throughout Scripture, encounters with God's glory are awe-inspiring:

- Isaiah cried, "Woe is me!" upon seeing the vision of God in the Temple. (Isaiah 6:5)

- Ezekiel fell on his face before the glory of the Lord. (Ezekiel 1:28)

- Daniel collapsed at the sound of God's voice. (Daniel 10:9)

These and other biblical examples show how we are not complacent in the presence of the living God—for He is eternal and infinite, while we are finite and temporal.

To experience the presence of God fully, the Lord must fashion new bodies for us that resemble Christ's resurrected body, as this author notes:

> The last stain of sin will have been washed from the souls of the redeemed, and they will be like Christ in holiness, while their bodies will be changed into a complete resemblance of his. Without a doubt, the glorified body of Jesus is the highest specimen of physical beauty and perfection in the universe, and the bodies of the saints are to be made just like it. The conformity will be so complete that the image of Christ will shine forth in the redeemed with resplendent glory through everlasting ages.[4]

There will be no more separation or distance between us—God will be with us in a way that far exceeds anything we can imagine.

The ultimate joy of heaven is not just the absence of sin and suffering, but also the glorious presence of God Himself. We will experience unending love, purpose, and worship, fully satisfied and surrounded by the light of His glory.

As we spend eternity with God in a world completely restored, our hope lies in entering into the fullness of a life that God originally intended for us when He created the heavens and the earth in the beginning.

At the heart of this eternal hope is Jesus Christ, the Savior who gave His life for the world and rose again in victory over death. In the new heaven and earth, the faith we've been walking by will give way to sight.

We will see Christ face to face—the same Jesus who walked on this earth among us, performing miracles, and bore our sin on the cross:

> But He *was* wounded for our transgressions, *He was* bruised for our iniquities; The chastisement for our peace *was* upon Him, And by His stripes we are healed. All we like sheep have gone astray; We have turned, every one, to his own way; And the Lord has laid on Him the iniquity of us all.   Isaiah 53:5–6

We will see God, our Creator, Jesus Christ, the Son of God along with His heavenly host—the angels who guarded us and carried out their Master's unseen purposes on our behalf.

We will join in eternal praise and worship of our holy God—for who He was, is, and always will be: I AM—our Creator, Redeemer, Lover, and Friend:

> You are worthy, O Lord, To receive glory and honor and power; For You created all things, And by Your will they exist and were created.   Revelation 4:11

Everything that has ever been created in heaven and earth will also be saying:

> Blessing and honor and glory and power *Be* to Him who sits on the throne, And to the Lamb, forever and ever!
> Revelation 5:13

Every sorrow will be healed, and every longing fulfilled. What we have yearned for in life will be realized fully in Him.

In the new heaven and new earth, no other pursuits or pleasures will be desired. In the fullness of our eternal joy, we will find complete satisfaction and fulfillment in God's presence forever.

➤ *Eternal Peace and Harmony with God*
God has always wanted our very best because He alone loves and cares for us with unmatched kindness, compassion, and tender mercy. He

knows us by name along with the exact number of hairs on our heads. (Matthew 10:30)

With love like this, how could we not trust Him—or long to be with Him forever? To grasp the magnitude of this blessed event fully, let's explore God's relationship with us from the beginning.

God has always desired to dwell with His people in harmonious fellowship. When the Lord arrives, He will make this an absolute reality:

> And I heard a loud voice from heaven saying, "Behold, the tabernacle of God is with men, and He will dwell with them, and they shall be His people.' God Himself will be with them and be their God. And God will wipe away every tear from their eyes; there shall be no more death, nor sorrow, nor crying. There shall be no more pain, for the former things have passed away." Revelation 21:3–4

Before the Fall, walking with God in the Garden of Eden was our intended destiny: living in a pure, loving, trusting relationship with Him, free from guilt, fear, and doubt forever. However, then came that most unfortunate event:

> And they heard the sound of the Lord God walking in the garden in the cool of the day, and Adam and his wife hid themselves from the presence of the Lord

> God among the trees of the garden.
> Genesis 3:8

Sin's awful byproducts: shame, guilt, and fear caused Adam and Eve to hide from the very presence of the Lord.

Instead of running to God, they ran from Him—and we've been running ever since.

Since the Fall, sin has separated us from God. He is holy—we are not. He is perfect—we are not. He is infinite—we are not. Before we can obtain any fellowship, these imperfections must be addressed:

> For as by one man's disobedience many were made sinners, so also by one Man's obedience many will be made righteous.
> Romans 5:19

We also read in Scripture:

> But now in Christ Jesus you who once were far off have been brought near by the blood of Christ. For He Himself is our peace, who has made both one, and has broken down the middle wall of separation.   Ephesians 2:13–14

As we explored earlier, God bestows Jesus' righteousness on us because of our faith in His vicarious sacrifice at Calvary. Our restoration is not by our works but by His grace alone:

> For by grace you have been saved through faith, and that not of yourselves; it is the gift of God, not of works, lest anyone should boast.   Ephesians 2:8–9

We could not climb back to God—He "bridged the gap" to us by revealing His redemptive plan—eternal peace and fellowship—requiring only our faith in Christ—not our works, to obtain it.

Faith in Christ results in our justification, which translates into eternal life and fellowship with God:

> Justification is a judicial or forensic act, i.e., an act of God as judge proceeding according to law, declaring that the sinner is just, i.e., that the law no longer condemns him, but acquits and pronounces him to be entitled to eternal life.[5]

We also can enjoy eternal peace and favor with God as promised in His Word:

> Therefore, having been justified by faith, we have peace with God through our Lord Jesus Christ, through whom also we have access by faith into this grace in which we stand, and rejoice in hope of the glory of God.   Romans 5:1–2.

Eternal peace and fellowship with God are ours today! All worry, anxiety, and fear are replaced with God's peace, calm, assurance, and ease. Ours is a perfect peace that we will have long after we see Him, which is our source of great comfort.

The moment we turned to Christ, God canceled our sin debt and restored our fellowship as His beloved children forever:

> But as many as received Him, to them He gave the right to become children of God, to those who believe in His name: who were born, not of blood, nor of the will of the flesh, nor of the will of man, but of God.   John 1:12–13

Through the blood of Jesus Christ, we can expect God's acceptance as He exchanges Jesus' perfect life for our imperfect one. When God looks at us, He sees redeemed children—made suitable for eternal fellowship with Him.

Much like condemned criminals, we stood before The Righteous Judge, condemned and helpless. Yet, His Righteous Son assumed our sin and penalty while we received His innocence and righteousness.

The Righteous Judge gave us a new identity, erasing our sin. Our old sin nature no longer defines us—instead, the righteousness of Christ and the power of His salvation define us:

Through his life, death, resurrection, and exaltation, come deliverance from the guilt and power of sin and the gift of new life through the indwelling Holy Spirit. So the believer is saved by Christ's work on the cross (Acts 4:12); he is being saved now by the work of the Holy Spirit, the Sanctifier (Philippians 2:12) and he looks forward to completed salvation in the life of the age to come. (1 Thessalonians 5:9, 1 Peter 1:5) [6]

Psalm 103:12 tells us, God has removed our sins as far as the east is separated from the west. He keeps no record of our past. Neither does He put us on probation until we "earn" His favor. Instead, He restores us to full fellowship without restriction and takes special delight in every detail of our lives.

Liberated from our sinful past, our guilt and shame cannot bind, enslave, or condemn us, nor can anything separate us from God's love forever:

> For I am persuaded that neither death nor life, nor angels nor principalities nor powers, nor things present nor things to come, nor height nor depth, nor any other created thing, shall be able to separate us from the love of God which is in Christ Jesus our Lord.   Romans 8:38–39

The massive weight of sin, guilt, and shame we've carried is gone. We now have a new identity and new destiny as completely forgiven children of God. We can freely fellowship with God—now and in glory.

While we prepare for that glorious day, we can participate in the "ministry of reconciliation" (2 Corinthians 5:18), by extending forgiveness and fostering an atmosphere of spiritual and emotional wholeness to others around us.

Since God has forgiven us, His Holy Spirit within us enables us to extend that same forgiveness and reconcile others as much as possible. Everyone benefits when we forgive and seek reconciliation as generously as our Lord has done for us.

To be in God's presence forever means that we regain what our ancestors lost—to dwell forever in perfect, unbroken communion with God—a state of complete joy, peace, and fulfillment.

This was the life God intended—close, peaceful, purposeful, and joyfully dependent on Him for everything. The tragedy of the Fall was the loss of fellowship, but it was fulfilled in Christ, and will be fully realized when He returns.

Peace and harmony with God signify the realization of our eternal hope: to be fully united with God without sin, separation, or death. As it was in the Garden, there will be no distance between God and His people; instead, there will be constant, intimate fellowship marked by love, holiness, and great glory.

> *Fellowship with Saints and Loved Ones*

The promise of reuniting with saints and loved ones in the new heaven and new earth is one of the greatest hopes of our shared Christian faith. It means we will spend eternity in a world free from sorrow and pain in the company of those we've cherished.

Alongside Christ, we'll also be with those we've loved and lost—family members, friends, and fellow believers who have gone before us.

Yet even more, we'll join a great gathering of saints from every generation. From the Old Testament, we'll meet Enoch who did not die but "walked with God." (Genesis 5:24) We will meet Abraham, the father of the faithful, for whom it is written:

> By faith Abraham obeyed when he was called to go out to the place which he would receive as an inheritance. And he went out, not knowing where he was going. By faith he dwelt in the land of promise as *in* a foreign country, dwelling in tents with Isaac and Jacob, the heirs with him of the same promise; for he waited for the city which has foundations, whose builder and maker *is* God.
> Hebrews 11:8–10

Moses, Joshua, Elijah, Esther, Ruth, Rahab, Jeremiah, Job, Daniel, King David, Solomon and so many other Old Testament lives that captivate and inspire us today—will become personal conversations when we meet and speak with them—by God's grace and mercy.

We will also encounter the Twelve Disciples and apostles like Peter, Paul, Andrew, James, Matthew, and John. We will meet Mary Magdalene, Mary and Joseph who nurtured the Christ child, Nicodemus, Lazarus, Mary and Martha, the Woman at the Well, Thomas, and others who walked with our Lord. They heard His teachings, received the Holy Spirit at Pentecost, started the New Testament Church, and spread the Gospel throughout the world.

Alongside them will be countless others across history celebrating together as one family—united by the cross of Jesus Christ.

This eternal reunion will be far more than a return to past relationships—it will be the total fulfillment of God's promise to make all things new.

No more tears, sadness, or parting. In that place, joy and worship will never end as we live in perfect harmony with God and one another—a family redeemed, restored, and rejoicing for all eternity.

> *The River of Life and the Tree of Life*

John's vision in Revelation gives us a glimpse of that moment when our Lord returns in glory:

> And he showed me a pure river of water of life, clear as crystal, proceeding from the throne of God and of the Lamb. In the middle of its street, and on either side of the river, was the tree of life, which bore twelve fruits, each tree yielding its fruit every month. The leaves of the tree were for the healing of the nations.
>
> Revelation 22:1–2

John's account reveals the complete and perfect nature of life in the new heaven and earth, where the River of Life and the Tree of Life stand as eternal symbols of God's abundant blessings for His people.

Sin and sorrow do not exist where there is unbroken communion with God. There, God's presence becomes our light, our joy, and our life—no more sorrow, no more longing.

It is where God's presence is the source of all joy and satisfaction, and where nothing causes sickness, disease, death, emotional pain, regret, or heartache. All of life's trials and burdens will be removed, and we will be freed from the pain caused by sin—our present human condition.

The River of Life and the Tree of Life represent our eternal state of health, wholeness, and abundant life—a restoration of Eden—graciously provided by God. For their healing symbolism points to the complete restoration of creation, a Paradise regained after the Fall.[7]

These symbols: the River of Life and the Tree of Life are not new. We see parallels in Genesis 2:8–10:

> The Lord God planted a garden eastward in Eden, and there He put the man whom He had formed. And out of the ground the Lord God made every tree grow that is pleasant to the sight and good for food. The tree of life *was* also in the midst of the garden, and the tree of the knowledge of good and evil. Now a river went out of Eden to water the garden, and from there it parted and became four riverheads.

Almost six-hundred years before John's vision in Revelation 22, God showed the prophet Ezekiel something very similar:

> Then he brought me back to the door of the temple; and there was water, flowing from under the threshold of the temple toward the east, for the front of the temple faced east; the water was flowing from under the right side of the temple, south of the altar. . . . Along the bank of the river, on this side and that, will grow all *kinds of* trees used for food; their leaves will not wither, and their fruit will not fail. They will bear fruit every month, because

their water flows from the sanctuary. Their fruit will be for food, and their leaves for medicine. Ezekiel 47:1, 12

One writer shares his thoughts about Ezekiel's vision:

> The leaves and fruits of these trees therefore possess supernatural powers. The fruits serve as food, i.e., for the maintenance of the life produced by the river of water; the leaves as medicine . . . for the healing of the sick and corrupt. . . . The figurative interpretation, or spiritual explanation, is moreover favoured by the analogy of the Scriptures. "Water," which renders the unfruitful land fertile, and supplies refreshing drink to the thirsty, is used in Scripture as a figure denoting blessing and salvation, which had been represented even in Paradise in the form of watering. . . . And lastly, the water of salvation also possesses the power to produce trees with leaves and fruits, by which the life called forth from death can be sustained and cured of all diseases. This is the meaning, according to the express statement of the text, of the trees with their never withering leaves, upon the banks of the river, and their fruits ripening every month.[8]

Jesus has something very profound to say about water and life:

> "But whoever drinks of the water that I shall give him will never thirst. But the water that I shall give him will become in him a fountain of water springing up into everlasting life." John 4:14

In the new heaven and new earth, God dwells visibly with His people. There will be no more death, no more mourning, and no more pain. The curse of sin is gone, the brokenness healed, and our longing for completeness is fulfilled.

We will share with God in a glorious and blissful fellowship for eternity—absent from all the pain and suffering we've ever experienced.

> ➢ Rest

Once we experience the glorification change that is coming, we will share in what the Bible calls rest. Hebrews 4 describes a rest that remains for the people of God—a rest that we have not yet fully entered, but must persevere in faith:

> There remains therefore a rest for the people of God. For he who has entered His rest has himself also ceased from his works as God *did* from His.
> Hebrews 4:9–10

Our eternal rest is not symbolic. It is the final destination of our redemption, the everlasting peace of God's presence, and the fulfillment of every promise to those who trust in Christ as Savior and Lord.

Even now, we have a foretaste spiritual rest—freedom from guilt and shame—yet we still journey through a fallen world.

The Holy Spirit dwells within us to comfort and guide us, yet we remain in a world marred by sin. Suffering, emptiness, temptation, and sorrow continue to haunt the experience of God's people. As the book of Hebrews warns us, we are not yet home.

Just as God's people wandered in the wilderness before entering the Promised Land, so the people of God today walk through a fallen world toward our final rest.

This is not rest in the sense of inactivity, but in the sense of complete, unhindered peace and joy. It is rest from striving, rest from fear, and rest from sorrow. Thus, our eternal rest is not some vague afterlife. It is the full realization of God's redemptive purpose for us, and His creation.

The phrase *eternal rest* captures a longing that has always lived within the human soul. In a world defined by constant motion, pressure, noise, and conflict, the promise of perfect and everlasting rest stands out as our beacon of hope.

It is the rest for which the human heart was made—life in the presence of God, where everything is as it should be, and nothing threatens or disturbs us. This rest is our unbroken communion with God that has been restored through Christ and made permanent.

We are to "strive to enter that rest." (Hebrews 4:11) God's eternal rest requires perseverance—a clinging to Christ that endures through hardship, temptation, and trial.

Many of the Israelites who left Egypt failed to enter their rest because of unbelief, despite witnessing God's power and provision. In their vivid example, we are warned not to harden our hearts and fall away:

> Therefore, as the Holy Spirit says: "Today, if you will hear His voice, Do not harden your hearts as in the rebellion, In the day of trial in the wilderness, Where your fathers tested Me, tried Me, And saw My works forty years. Therefore I was angry with that generation, And said, 'They always go astray in *their* heart, And they have not known My ways.' So I swore in My wrath, 'They shall not enter My rest.'"
> Hebrews 3:7–11

Our striving is not earning—it's enduring; holding to the One who holds us. It is the persistent trust in God that moves forward even when the path is hard. We strive because we believe in Him and His promises, and we endure because what lies ahead is better than anything the world can offer.

Eternal rest is not an abstract hope; it is our very goal of salvation. It is the joy that no grief can touch, and the home that will never be lost:

> In My Father's house are many mansions; if *it were* not *so,* I would have told you. I go to prepare a place for you. And if I go and prepare a place for you, I will come again and receive you to Myself; that where I am, *there* you may be also.
> John 14:2–3

This future rest also gives shape and meaning to the present journey. Knowing what lies ahead helps us endure with patience and hope. It gives purpose to our obedience, strength to our perseverance, and peace in our waiting.

Eternal rest reassures us that pain, struggle, and death are not the end, and that since Jesus has overcome, we too will overcome, and every tear will be wiped away by the hand of God Himself.

Our eternal hope as Christians is both personal and universal in nature—we will be transformed individually, yet God will renew all of creation.

God is with His people, and the rest that remains will be seen in the restoration of all things under the reign of Christ forever.

Therefore, we wait. We strive. We hope—and we persevere. The rest that remains for the people of God is certain, secured by the finished work of

Christ at the cross. It is coming—and when it does, it will be more glorious than we could ever imagine.

Preparing for the Change Awaiting Us
We find peace when we seek and anticipate the magnificent spiritual blessings that are hidden from the world but promised to us in eternity:

> While we do not look at the things which are seen, but at the things which are not seen. For the things which are seen *are* temporary, but the things which are not seen *are* eternal.   2 Corinthians 4:18

Our chief aim is to dwell in our glorious, heavenly home, where "the wicked shall cease from troubling, and the weary shall be at rest." (Job 3:17) The hopes and desires of all believers everywhere are found in this central expectation—to live in heaven with Christ and God.

There, we have perfect understanding of the work and ways of God. We no longer "know in part," but will know Him as we are known by Him, and we will "see Him as He is" in His full majestic splendor.

Jesus is preparing a place where holiness, glory, love, rest, and unspeakable joy abound beyond our imagination. Our eternal home—a place of glorification—is where we will bask in God's full, unfiltered presence, without sin, pain, or disease:

> So when this corruptible shall have put on incorruption, and this mortal shall have put on immortality, then shall be brought to pass the saying that is written, death is swallowed up in victory.
>
> 1 Corinthians 15:54 (AKJV)

It is a place of eternal blessing and satisfaction—beyond anything we have seen or heard here on earth, as the Word declares:

> Then I heard a voice from heaven saying to me, "Write: 'Blessed *are* the dead who die in the Lord from now on.' " "Yes," says the Spirit, "that they may rest from their labors, and their works follow them."
>
> Revelation 14:13

Standing on the observation deck at the Grand Canyon can be a breathtaking experience—just like hearing the roar of Niagara Falls or walking among stately Redwoods. White, sandy beaches, tropical sunrises, and pastel-colored sunsets captivate us and stir our souls.

Even the world's greatest wonders—grand canyons, waterfalls, and sunsets—are mere shadows compared to one split-second in eternity. This world is not our eternal home. We are pilgrims and strangers, journeying through a place that is passing away as we press toward a far better, celestial home.

God has placed within us a deep spiritual longing to dwell in His presence forever—and He will fulfill that longing completely.

While we wait for the glorious day when Christ fulfills all His promises, let us live lives that honor the Lord—so we too may echo the words of faith and victory:

> I have fought the good fight, I have finished the race, I have kept the faith. Finally, there is laid up for me the crown of righteousness, which the Lord, the righteous Judge, will give to me on that Day, and not to me only but also to all who have loved His appearing.
> 2 Timothy 4:7–8

Completing the Circle
I, too, have been in preparation for that glorious day of change, just as the Word of God exhorts:

> *I had fainted*, unless I had believed to see the goodness of the LORD in the land of the living. Wait on the LORD: be of good courage, and he shall strengthen thine heart: wait, I say, on the LORD.
> Psalm 27:13–14

Thus, here is where I share the rest of my story.

She lay near death that night. I gently kissed her forehead and whispered, "Thank you for being a great mom."

She would be with Jesus in a few moments, but her precious memory would resonate in my heart for years to come. Before meeting my wife, Mom was my best friend, and she is one for whom these words seem fitting:

> Charm *is* deceitful and beauty *is* passing,
> But a woman *who* fears the Lord, she shall
> be praised.   Proverbs 31:30

Grandma and Dad had gone to be with the Lord several years before, and I still miss them terribly. They made a tremendous imprint on my life.

I thank God for being raised in their loving home, hearing their inspirational stories, receiving their wise and godly counsel, and most importantly, having them introduce me to Jesus Christ.

They supported me when I married, started a family, completed my undergraduate degree, and became an ordained minister.

I wasn't looking to marry when my college classmate invited me to the Sunday morning worship service at his church. I accepted his invitation, assuming it would be a normal worship experience.

However, once the services began—I saw her. I was instantly captivated by her radiance as the Lord used her in leading music during the service.

She sang and spoke like someone who knew the Lord and wanted to share Him with others.

For me, it was "love at first sight" when the Lord whispered to me, *"She's the one!"*

These prophetic words have proven to be true over the years:

> *He who* finds a wife finds a good *thing,*
> And obtains favor from the LORD.
> Proverbs 18:22

To my wife and me, Matthew 28's Great Commission meant: *"Go ye therefore!"* and we went wherever we could to serve the Lord.

With our combined gifts of music, preaching, teaching, serving, and leadership, we traveled around the country serving in churches. We supported the pastors and ministry leaders in their ministries wherever we went by serving in the background so they could lead in the foreground.

After a while, although we were both very active and productive, we sensed a spiritual restlessness as the Lord led us to return home.

We arrived home and continued our church service and my bi-vocational work. However, within two years, Dad went to be with Jesus, and I found myself responsible for three households: Mom's, Grandma's, and my own.

The Lord began to reshape my understanding of what my "ministry" would be. Initially, I believed I would be a missionary or serve in traditional pastoral ministry. Yet, I served bi-vocationally. Then it began to dawn on me that "ministry" did not necessarily mean pastoring a church, going into the far corners of the world, or even holding a full-time ministry position.

Ministry also applies to my parents—serving them faithfully—repaying the love and care they unselfishly and sacrificially gave me over the years. This is exactly what Scripture calls us to do:

> Honor your father and your mother, that your days may be long upon the land which the LORD your God is giving you.
> Exodus 20:12

I wasn't looking for a "long life." I wanted to do right, and the Lord's favor soon became evident. He blessed the ministry and us as I served as a church minister and program administrator.

I had given up on completing my education, realizing how difficult it was to finance seminary. Many years had passed since I finished my undergraduate degree, and I was busy working and raising a family.

The Lord sent a dear brother in Christ who covered my tuition and books, allowing me to complete my graduate seminary degree. Then the

Lord blessed us financially while opening the door for me to finish my doctoral degree a few years later.

For what the Lord performed on our behalf, I am still utterly astounded. *What an amazing God*.

> Now to Him who is able to do exceedingly abundantly above all that we ask or think, according to the power that works in us, to Him *be* glory in the church by Christ Jesus to all generations, forever and ever. Amen.   Ephesians 3:20–21

Those years I spent in the classroom while working and serving at church and my family gave me a profound appreciation for learning. If I could recapture those moments today, I'd invest more in those invigorating settings.

Shortly after I graduated, Mom decided to downsize from our three-story family dwelling to a smaller place in a rural area across the country. She and Grandma wanted to be closer to extended family while enjoying a slower pace of life, far from the hustle and bustle of the metropolis.

The ministry now became "in home care" as my wife and I followed shortly thereafter. We were "empty nesters," and my bi-vocational ministry evolved as I transitioned into a full-time role as senior chaplain at a state correctional facility, while we continued to serve both the local church and the broader community.

After fifteen years and Mom's passing, which left a huge hole in our lives, we both sensed the Lord leading us to return home—and closer to family, once again.

We obeyed—but soon found ourselves in another season of unexpected grief. Within a very short span, both of my wife's parents passed away. Then she lost a close sibling along with other family members and loved ones in rapid succession.

Yet, we sensed God's refining work, bringing us closer to Him amidst our trials and sorrows:

> Beloved, do not think it strange concerning the fiery trial which is to try you, as though some strange thing happened to you, but rejoice to the extent that you partake of Christ's sufferings, that when His glory is revealed, you may also be glad with exceeding joy.
> 1 Peter 4:12–13

The Lord gave us the strength to survive the crucible of grief, but now we face the ultimate challenge—time.

With aging, we feel we have come full circle as our children now look after us. It seems strange to be on the receiving end of the advice, counsel, and care we gave so often.

At first, it felt like I was giving away my control. Then I realized that control is an illusion; I have no control—*God is in control*—and He is always at work, moving me toward fulfilling His perfect plan:

> To everything *there is* a season, A time for every purpose under heaven.
> Ecclesiastes 3:1

The Lord remains sovereign, and in control. To Him, I am just as vital in this quieter fall/winter season as I was in earlier days in the pulpit, or prison, the classroom, or at my computer workstation.

My desire today is to finish well, by fulfilling the tasks and duties He gives me—until I see Jesus face to face and hear Him say, "*Well done!*"

Even so, it has not been very easy arriving at this season of life—especially having to say goodbye to a world I loved, which possesses so many cherished memories.

A world that was familiar, comforting, and deeply engrained into my daily experience has been replaced with one that feels foreign to me in almost every way possible.

Everything now feels profoundly unfamiliar—our values and culture, the ways we relate and communicate, our approach to health, work, worship, and even the pace and priorities of daily life.

Sin, Satan, and selfish pursuits have reshaped the social and political landscape in ways I never could have imagined. The world I once recognized and felt comfortable in now feels distant and foreign—at times, almost like an alien planet.

Jesus spoke of this happening on the earth, but I never thought I'd see it in my day:

> And because lawlessness will abound, the love of many will grow cold.
> Matthew 24:12

Nevertheless, the irony is that having others express care for us with the same tenderness we showed has become one of our greatest blessings. It's the living evidence of God's faithfulness from one generation to the next.

After years of providing, we now find ourselves on the receiving end. This transition—from provider to receiver—serves as a reminder that God is still at work.

In ministry and in parenthood, we spent years "pouring into" the lives of others. We traveled, served, taught, counseled, cooked meals, paid bills, fixed what was broken, and held things together through faith and prayer. Now, we must allow others to do the same for us.

This full-circle moment goes beyond the aspect of aging to reveal the unfolding of God's perfect plan for us in ways we had not anticipated.

So yes; this new role stretches our faith, and our preparation for the Lord's return now requires us to trust the Lord in ways we never have before.

We trust God where we once leaned on ourselves, and we accept help from others when needed—with grace and thanksgiving:

> In everything give thanks; for this is the will of God in Christ Jesus for you.
> 1 Thessalonians 5:18

I can rest in what the Lord wants to do in and through others on my behalf, when I can't do for myself. God is sovereign and will not forsake me in my old age as the Psalmist observes:

> O God, You have taught me from my youth; And to this *day* I declare Your wondrous works. Now also when *I am* old and grayheaded, O God, do not forsake me, Until I declare Your strength to *this* generation, Your power to everyone *who* is to come. Psalm 71:17–18

I understand that even at this age, we can still minister effectively and live for God's glory by learning to receive care with grace. Though we may no longer serve as prominently or as often as before, our lives still matter—and the Lord continues to use us for His glory.

In the meantime, I remain confident in God's perfect plan:

> For this reason I also suffer these things; nevertheless I am not ashamed, for I know whom I have believed and am persuaded that He is able to keep what I have committed to Him until that Day.
> 2 Timothy 1:12

The King is Coming

At His coming, those who have died in the Lord will be raised, and we who are alive will join the Lord, His Saints, and our departed loved ones. This glorious reunion is our great, eternal hope. Until then, we are comforted by the promise that we will see the Son of Man coming in the clouds with great power and glory.

Yet, our Christian faith is not merely about a distant future, because it transforms how we live today. We do not cling to empty hopes, but to a living faith that brings spiritual abundance, peace, and purpose here and now.

Our eternal life begins the moment we receive Christ and continues unbroken even through death into eternity. This hope shapes our values, our mission, and our witness—both in this life and far into the next.

When our earthly journey ends and the Lord calls us home from labor to eternal reward, we will experience the culmination of His redemptive plan. There, the weary will find perfect rest, and the faithful will be free from sorrow, fear, and pain.

In the new heaven and new earth, we will dwell in God's radiant presence, where sin, suffering, and disease are no more. This promised resurrection and final transformation—our glorification—is the completion of our salvation. God will give us immortal, glorified bodies, conformed to the likeness of Christ's resurrected body. We will behold His face and fullness, transformed into His image.

No amount of human effort or self-righteousness can earn God's favor. Only the atoning sacrifice of Jesus Christ on Calvary secures our salvation and eternal destiny. Our faith in Christ transforms our identity, shapes our conduct, and secures our eternal hope.

All will stand before Christ one day. For some, He will be Righteous Judge—but for us—our Blessed Hope, and eternal reward.

Since we fully trust in the One who holds our future in His faithful and loving hands, let us therefore live with eager expectation and unwavering hope, standing firm in our faith.

Our Redeemer is coming—*and very soon!*

Notes

[1] See: Cecil B. Murphey, ed., "Eschatology (The Last Things)," in *The Dictionary of Biblical Literacy: Essential Information on the Bible, Biblical Culture, and the Church* (Nashville: Thomas Nelson, 1989), 494—508.

[2] Wayne Grudem, "D. All Evangelicals Agree in the Final Results of Christ's Return," in *Systematic Theology: An Introduction to Biblical Doctrine*, chap. 54, "The Return of Christ: When and How?" (Leicester, England: Inter-Varsity Press; Grand Rapids, MI: Zondervan, 1994)1094—5.

[3] "XVIII. Of the World to Come," in *The New Hampshire Baptist Confession*, in William L. Lumpkin, *Baptist Confessions of Faith*, rev. ed. (Valley Forge, PA: Judson Press, 1969), 367.

[4] James Madison Pendleton, "Chapter XXVIII: The Resurrection," in *Christian Doctrines: A Compendium of Theology*, 23rd printing (Valley Forge, PA: Judson Press, 1976), 385.

[5] Charles Hodge, "Chapter XVII, Justification," sec. 2, "Justification is a Forensic Act," in *Systematic Theology*, 3rd printing, vol. 3 (Peabody, MA: Hendrickson, 2003), 119.

[6] J. D. Douglas, Walter A. Elwell, and Peter Toon, "Salvation," in *The Concise Dictionary of the Christian Tradition: Doctrine, Liturgy, History* (Grand Rapids, MI: Regency Reference Library, 1989), 335—6.

[7] A.T. Robertson, "Chapter XXII," in *Word Pictures in the New Testament, Vol. 6: The General Epistles and The Revelation of John* (Nashville: Sunday School Board of the Southern Baptist Convention; Grand Rapids, MI: Baker Book House, 1933), 479–80.

[8]C.F.Keil, "Chapter xlvii. 1—12: The River of Water of Life," in *Commentary on the Old Testament* by C.F. Keil and F. Delitzsch, vol. 9 *Ezekiel, Daniel*, reprint (Grand Rapids, MI: William B. Eerdmans Publishing Company, 1985), 360—61.

About the Author

Throughout his life, Floyd Bland has served in various ministry roles, including teacher, administrator, chaplain, and pastor. Now, through Not Of The World Ministries, Inc., he offers biblically based, interactive models for Christian living. To learn more about Not Of The World Ministries, Inc., visit their website at https://notwm.org/.

Floyd's most recent works include The Christian Heritage: God's Answers for a Searching World, Radical Forgiveness Through the Eyes of Jesus, Five Things Every Christian Must Know, and *Oh for the Joy! Forgiven and Free in Christ.* Other titles include *The Last Words of Jesus to His Disciples: Enduring Lessons of Faith, Hope, and Love* and *Tribulation Worketh Patience: Living Triumphantly through Faith and Enduring Hope.*

Floyd received his bachelor's degree from the California Baptist University, his master's degree from the Berkeley School of Theology, and his doctorate from the Pacific School of Religion.

Floyd is married to his best friend and lifelong partner, and together they have two grown children and a grandson.

www.ingramcontent.com/pod-product-compliance
Lightning Source LLC
Chambersburg PA
CBHW052144070526
44585CB00017B/1974